American Art
Collector

Volume 1, Book 1

Western States

Open to artists residing in:
Alaska, Arizona, California, Hawaii,
Nevada, Oregon and Washington

Juried competition of new art under $5000
Published quarterly by region
West, Central, Northeast, and Southeast

ALCOVE BOOKS
Berkeley, California

American Art
Collector

PUBLISHED QUARTERLY
$29 for four issues annually
subscribe@alcovebooks.net

Volume 1, Book 1 - Western States

Editor:
Tom Palmer

Assistant Editors:
DeWitt Cheng, Aileen Kim,
Laura Lea, Kimberly Stewart.

Thanks to Clay Jensen and
Virginia Breier for helping select
from over 300 artist submissions.

ALCOVE BOOKS
930 Dwight Way, #7
Berkeley, CA 94710
www.alcovebooks.net
510.644.3534

ISBN 0-9721890-2-5
Printed in Hong Kong.

Front cover:
Hillside Harvest, Beverly Wilson

Back cover:
Rutile, Ian Gilula

Right, top:
Chinese Checkers, James Gleeson

Right, bottom:
Idly Wood, Jane Burton

In the fragmented market for contemporary fine art and craft, hundreds of galleries, festivals and open studios display the efforts of thousands of artists—each seeking to communicate a unique vision of beauty and meaning.

It is my pleasure to work with many of these artists, to present a juried selection of new American art in four annual editions.

This debut issue includes artists from California, Oregon, Washington and Arizona. Many participate in well-known festivals, others choose only limited gallery representation. Contact information is provided for both the artist and their venues.

Showing individually-created pieces priced below $5000 in a variety of media, *American Art Collector* should interest both the casual and experienced buyer of original art.

Tom Palmer

CONTENTS

PART ONE: 2-D   **Page**

Drawing   4-91

Painting

Photography

Printmaking

PART TWO: 3-D

Ceramics   92

Glass   124

Jewelry   137

Metal   151

Textiles   162

Wood   167

INDEX

Venues   184

Artists   190

Photo Credits   191

Kent Alexander

Oakland, CA
www.kentalexander.com • 510.568.3183

THE COMMITTEE. Oil on canvas. 24" x 24"

"When I look in a mirror, I see many people—not in a schizophrenic way, but rather the interrelationships of my various 'selves'. Suddenly, I had no reason to do anything except explore my image very directly—no distractions, just conversations with my self."
Venues: SFMOMA Artists Gallery, Fresh Paint, Art Source LA.

Gilbert Amavisca

Sacramento, CA
gfamavisca@yahoo.com • 916.601.2336

UNTITLED. Oil on board. 15" x 19"

"I have always been inspired by the landscape of Northern California. I interpret these scenes with representational paintings in oil, using bold color and expressive brush strokes." Venues: Mill Valley Fall Art Festival, Barton Gallery, Elliot Fouts Gallery.

Amos Amit

Los Angeles, CA
lsamit@aol.com • 323.938.6957

NIGHT & DAY. Batik on cloth. 34" x 44"

"The uniqueness of the batik process and the warmth of the fabric inspire in me an emotional connection to the subject. Color and texture excite and animate my creativity. Although my art may range from primitive to free-flowing modern, the unifying thread is a passionate identification with the vision."

VINEYARD PATTERNS. Watercolor, tempera. 15" x 19.5"

"Through forty years of painting, the landscape has been the basis of my work. Close association with nature, careful observation, and quiet attention are an integral part of each painting. The image begins with the landscape, yet design and feeling are the true subjects." Venues: Affaire in the Gardens, Rest of the Best, Palo Alto Festival of the Arts.

ISLAND FEVER. Oil on canvas. 16" x 20"

"I explore the balance between natural and human-made form, the tension between biomorphic and geometric. The use of thick oil and spontaneous brush movement creates a three-dimensional effect by using heavy atmosphere and strong light."
Venues: Howard Mandville Gallery, New Masters Gallery, Thomas Reynolds Gallery.

Patricia Blau

San Rafael, CA
pblau@sonic.net • 415.258.9325

CALA T-BONE. Oil on board. 11.75" x 14"

"Painting is a physical manifestation of my seeing. This series follows the centuries-old tradition of still life—in it, I am focusing my attention on objects which I believe have become 'invisible' to us." Venue: Artworks Downtown.

STUDIO STILL LIFE #11. Watercolor on paper. 30" x 22"

"My recent still life watercolors explore a merging of Asian and European aesthetics. My feelings for the natural world, personal symbolism, and a fascination with pattern and color are fused in a dynamic and involving pictorial space that challenges the perspective of the viewer." Venues: Anne Bradford Gallery, Hunters Point Open Studios.

Louis Bording

San Francisco, CA
www.abstractart4u.com • 415.296.0342

UNTITLED #744. Mixed media on acrylic. 48" x 48"

"Eons have passed since someone picked up a burned stick and rubbed it against a cave wall. Man's fascination with art has not changed, only the materials. There is magic in a process using a mark, a line or a color, that can represent reality or an image with no basis in reality." Venues: ALC Designs, Virtual Art Solutions, ArtMatch.

Janine Brown

Berkeley, CA
jstudio2@aol.com • 510.548.6946

FOLDING/UNFOLDING #4. Acrylic on washi. 36" x 24"

"I am exploring how color affects the shifting paradox of surface pattern and illusionary space. In this acrylic painting on *washi*, I combine stamping with handmade stamps and collage. The subtle textures of the papers add richness to the process."
Venues: SFMOMA Artists Gallery, LIMN Gallery, Art Concepts.

Ray Buffalo

San Francisco, CA
ray@raybuffalo.com • 415.641.6136

MATADOR. Oil on linen. 36" x 32"

"Abstract painting can feel strikingly familiar yet provocatively vague—that's the territory I explore. I concern myself with dichotomies: composition and decomposition, balance and imbalance, deliberation and spontaneity. Good paintings maintain the dynamic equilibrium of opposites." Venues: SFMOMA Artists Gallery, San Francisco Open Studios.

Kathleen T. Carr

Sebastopol, CA
www.kathleencarr.com • 707.829.5649

LANE, MOLOKAI. Black & white infrared photograph. 7.5" x 10"

"I mostly work with alternative photographic processes such as Polaroid transfers, SX-70 manipulations, and black and white infrared, often hand coloring the images. These processes allow me to express a more subjective vision than with straight photographic prints." Venues: ARTrails Open Studios, Alinder Studio Gallery, Packard Reath Gallery.

Amelia Chao

Oakhurst, CA
www.lightscapegallery.net • 559.641.7771

EYE OF SORROW. Photograph. 8" x 10" or 20" x 24"

"I use a large format camera to capture the best light, and the fluid forms, textures
and tonal changes effected by water, cloud, fog, and wind. Ilfochrome, hand-made
in my darkroom, is my medium of choice for its longevity, sharpness and depth."
Venues: Mill Valley Fall Art Festival, Palo Alto Festival of the Arts, Salem Art Fair.

Belinda Chlouber

San Mateo, CA
www.tenfingers.com • 650.578.9261

INTO THE WOODS. Encaustic on panel. 9" x 11.5"

"By layering paint, I weave symbolism, abstraction and narrative imagery into scenes hidden within my work. Humanity's relationship to the environment has been a rich source of inspiration and, at times, distress for me. Paintings' stories never end—they begin again with every person who views them." Venues: SFMOMA Artists Gallery, Atelier 31 Gallery.

Carolyn Cole

Portland, OR
carolyncole@comcast.net • 503.292.7914

REVERB. Mixed media on canvas. 37" x 37"

"My paintings hover between consciousness and intuition, combining emotional content, observation, exploration, and reinvention. Layers of paper and paint accumulate, covering earlier marks and passages, scraping away what came before." Venues: Alysia Duckler Gallery, Cohen Rese Gallery, Highlands Sculpture Gallery.

Mitchell Confer

Menlo Park, CA
www.conferart.com • 415.822.2833

HILL SIDE. Mixed media on linen. 22" x 28"

"I focus on presenting everyday objects or places in radically different ways, exploring shapes, colors and a wide range of materials. My creative process centers on experimenting with each of these areas to construct images both familiar and abstract to the viewer." Venue: San Francisco Open Studios.

Melinda L. Cootsona

Menlo Park, CA
www.mlcstudios.com • 650.566.1528

INTO THE FOREST. Oil on canvas. 40" x 30"

"In my painting there is often a fine line between the real and the abstract. I often play with the transparency and opacity of the oil paint to achieve layering and depth. My work is influenced by the Society of Six and the Bay Area figurative artists."
Venues: Eriksen Gallery, Pieces Gallery, Silicon Valley Open Studios.

THE MIDNIGHT DANCE-3. Acrylic on canvas. 48" x 48"

"Warm colors, shapes and lines drive my work. I like to work in series, and enjoy being playful with the subjects I have in mind. I work with acrylics, often incorporating resin, Polaroid transfer or collage in my paintings." Venues: Pieces Gallery, The Blue Studio, San Francisco Open Studios.

Jan Davidson

Olema, CA
www.jandavidson.com • 415.663.0328

JUST BEFORE WAKING, 2. Acrylic on canvas. 30" x 24"

In my recent work, the subject is often the internal landscape. I combine representational and abstract styles to explore how thoughts influence perception—how what is observed and experienced is construed or misconstrued by beliefs and preconceived ideas.
Venues: Mill Valley Fall Arts Festival, Artisans Gallery, Pointe Reyes Open Studios.

Monica Denevan

San Francisco, CA
www.monicadenevan.com • 415.515.2871

MACHETE (Caura River, Venezuela). Silver gelatin print. 15" x 15"

"My photographs begin with the personal connections made with people in remote areas of Asia and Latin America. The images become a relationship between people and their environment. I look to photograph the extraordinary resonance humming within lives most ordinary." Venues: San Francisco Open Studios, Hunters Point Open Studios.

N.A. Diaman

San Francisco, CA
nadiaman@aol.com • 415.775.6143

BUDDIES. Photograph. 24" x 36"

"Art for me offers a glimpse into another reality. I look for interesting images or
compositions in everyday life to photograph, finding beauty within both sparse
simplicity and lush elegance. I am especially drawn to vivid colors. Above all, I strive
to present a fresh photographic vision."

Reif Erickson

Auburn, CA
www.reif.com • 530.887.9565

SUMMIT VIEW. Pastel. 11" x 15"

"I touch the earth with my heart and paint the spirit of the land. My paintings are more than pigment and paper. They are light, and heart, and I paint the heart of the land." Venues: Mill Valley Fall Art Festival, Vault Gallery, Youngman Gallery.

Karen Ruth Evenson

San Diego, CA
krephoto@earthlink.net • 619.269.0324

ESCHER'S BEETLES. Ilfochrome print. 20" x 16"

"Contact with medieval art convinces me of the power of symbolism in artistic imagery. I compose still lifes as iconic cruciforms that contain form and frame. Beyond these confines lie objects that symbolize other realms of existence and other dimensions of time and space." Venues: SFMOMA Artists Gallery, Bassetti Fine Art.

Todd H. Friedlander

Oakland, CA
www.toddfriedlander.com • 415.244.4259

PIPES (Butler, California). Photograph. 11" x 14"

"I am struck by the knowledge that everything is changing. A photograph records a unique place and time—the memory of what I was thinking and feeling when snapping the shutter. Photographs evoke an entirely different feeling or memory for the viewer." Venues: SFMOMA Artists Gallery, SF Open Studios, Buy Fine Art Before You're 60 Show.

Greg Gawlowski

San Francisco, CA
www.fourseasonspress.com

MAROON LAKE. Photograph. 34" x 39"

"As a travel photographer, I search for beautiful scenes that also demonstrate themes I strive to communicate. I feel our society's pace is increasing at a monumental level, and my goal is to create calming, peaceful, and healing images." Venues: Mill Valley Fall Art Festival, Sacramento Art Festival.

TWO ERAS. Etching. 9" x 3.5"

"Instead of portraying people, I portay their environments. I mostly use hard-ground monochrome etching. My subjects range from representational urban portraits to flowing, abstract forms. Most of the work is done through crosshatching and stippling."
Venues: ACCI Gallery, Freehand, Eriksen Gallery.

Paul D. Gibson

San Francisco, CA
www.pdgarts.com • 415.751.7949

TEA PARTY. Pastel on 100% rag. 36" x 36"

"The work I produce reveals the hidden life and energy of ordinary objects. I try to approach each subject with imagination and a sense of discovery. I use spatial and verbal ambiguity in each work—producing a story behind each subject."
Venues: Andrea Schwartz Gallery, George Krevsky Gallery, Allan Stone Gallery.

CHINESE CHECKERS. Acrylic on paper. 30" x 38"

"As an artist, I am an observer of the people around me. I find beauty in the everyday people that go unobserved by many. I work in watercolor and acrylic on paper. Drawing and design are very important facets in my work." Venues: Sausalito Art Festival, San Francisco Open Studios, Ggallery.biz.

Sylvia Gonzalez

Petaluma, CA
www.sylviagonzalez.com • 707.781.6977

GREEN APPLE ON RED. Pastel. 25" x 38"

"Simple composition and bold contrast of color are what my work is about. Playing with color and watching light move and change is a meditation for me. I use pastels primarily for the rich, soft color, but enjoy mixing media as well, such as monotype and collage."
Venues: The Gardener, CFA Gallery, ARTrails Open Studios.

Wendy Gruber

Sausalito, CA
www.wendygruber.com

FOG & GRASSES. Pastel, acrylic. 25" x 20"

"In my *plein air* landscapes, I tease out an exchange between the strokes and colors of acrylic washes and pastels. Rather than documenting a scene, I focus on the essence of the place at that moment. I want the grasses I paint to keep blowing after the piece is finished." Venues: Sausalito Art Festival, Marin Art Festival, ICB Building Shows.

Donny Hahn

South San Francisco, CA
donny@donnyhahn.com

CRY FOR A SHADOW. Oil on canvas. 28" x 36"

"The essential ingredients in my work have always been light and color. I work in open air, trying to capture the impression of nature with minimal detail. Creating these field sketches of light and color are the cornerstone of my paintings. I take a simple approach to form, with a bold approach to color." Venue: Mill Valley Fall Art Festival.

BEANSTALK SKY. Oil on paper. 25.5" x 19.5"

"I use oil paint because it is a visceral and surprising medium; color and brushstroke
are my catalysts. In the process of making marks, putting colors down next to each
other, defining areas of the surface, a story is told." Venues: Steel Gallery, ZYT Gallery,
Hunters Point Open Studios.

Fain Hancock

Benicia, CA
fainh@earthlink.net

IT'S WHAT ALL THE GIRLS ARE WEARING. Oil, lipstick on canvas. 30" x 40"

"Growing up in Texas, I was often told by my mother and other women relatives to be lady-like, yet strong and independent. My titles are often from direct quotes. I mine the powerful truth of my female experience. These paintings are emotional landscapes and a record of thoughts forming." Venues: Hang Gallery, Greenwood Chebithes Gallery.

Wynne Hayakawa

San Francisco, CA
wynne@netwiz.net • 415.641.5127

SIENNA CIRCLES. Oil on canvas. 40" x 48"

"I want to create a place where we can exist and breathe for a while. Some of my paintings are recognizable landscapes. Other pieces are stripes of multi-layered color. I hope to make a vibration of color that resonates within us. I paint in oil because I find oil paint beautiful." Venues: Andrea Schwartz, Dolphin Gallery, Hunters Point Open Studios.

Clinton C. Hensley

Albany, CA
510.526.9279

BAND-AID. Acrylic on wood. 36" x 18"

"I consider my work to be acts of reconciliation with materials, nature, and environment. My work can be highly labor-intensive, however, the result tends to be visually unimposing." Venues: Worth Ryder Gallery, Southern Exposure.

Jonn Herschend

San Francisco, CA
www.jonnherschend.com • 415.861.8416

THE WAY I WAS TOLD IT WOULD BE. Mixed media on panel. 29" x 16"

"I was raised in a midwestern theme park, and have always wanted to pull people into worlds that are outside the everyday. I try to create paintings that tell stories about maudlin events in a stream of conscious manner." Venues: Hang Gallery, Tag Gallery.

Bruce Hopkins

Berkeley, CA
www.bkhopkins.com • 510.841.4277

SPACE 6 #1D. Digital.

"This image is part of a series of 260 digitally-created compositions titled 'Space.' Using only curves, circles and pure hues combined with rhythm, harmony and movement, 'Space' expresses the 'Music of the Spheres.' Offered as wide-format digital *giclée* prints in limited editions." Venues: Graton Gallery, Plaza Arts Gallery, East Bay Open Studios.

Patrick Howe

Seattle, WA
www.patrickhowe.com • 206.860.8031

TUSCANY MEADOW. Oil on canvas. 30" x 20"

"My wish is to express artistic excellence."
Venues: Serendipity Fine Arts, Rhodes Stringfellow, Bellevue Art Museum Fair.

John Claude Hundt

San Francisco, CA
jchundt@aol.com • 415.550.1118

BEDLINGTON. Collage, mixed media. 36" x 36"

"My paintings are built up using collage materials collected over the past ten years. From there it is a process of subconscious doodles and images representing social commentary and the absurd, and are occasionally auto-biographical." Currently seeking gallery representation.

MORCEAUX D'ESPACES XX. Oil on thirteen canvases. 35" x 24"

"The series *Morceaux d'Espaces* consists of assemblages of small oil paintings. Juxtaposing canvases painted individually (often weeks apart) facilitates the questioning and playing with the conventional pictorial signs system and disrupts any intentional symbolism. But ultimately painting is a dialogue with color." Venue: SF Open Studios.

Stephanie Jucker

San Rafael, CA
sjucker@sbcglobal.net • 415.460.6795

BRIAR ROSE. Encaustic on canvas. 24" x 36"

"Using female imagery from fairy tales, religion, and personal experience, I am exploring
the disparity between society's expectations of women and their reality—echoed by
an encaustic technique of contrasting textures created using oil paint, wax, and sand."
Venues: Art Works Downtown, Marin Open Studios, Hang Art.

LISTENING TO ELLIS. Oil on canvas. 24" x 20"

"Little stories about humans as they are affected by music are my favorite subject matter. Oil paint is my favorite medium because it will still look good long after I am pushing up petunias." Venues: Sausalito Art Festival, New York Art Expo, *Biennale Internazionale D'ell Arte Contemporane*.

Walter Kennedy

San Francisco, CA
www.wckennedy.com • 415.647.9065

S.F. DRYDOCKS #2. Silver gelatin print. 8" x 8"

"I have always been interested in showing the passage of time in photographs. This piece is from a series I have been working on for a few years near the drydocks. I am fascinated by how the night light interacts with the water, the ships and the structures." Venues: SFMOMA Artists Gallery, Freddie Fong Gallery, San Francisco Open Studios.

Casey Klahn

Davenport, WA
kcklahn@msn.com • 509.796.3277

RED BARN WITH RAMP. Pastel. 12.75" x 9.25"

"My pastels are sketched on-site, then redrawn from memory to provide a degree of separation from the representational. Images are from the American western landscape, but while painting I am thinking of blocks of color and shapes." Venues: Spectrum Studio, Spokane ArtFest, Northwest Museum of Art & Culture Store.

Ines Kramer

Oakland, CA
inesco8@aol.com

POOL. Mixed media on paper. 10" x 10"

"Exploring places where manmade elements meet nature, I create loose armatures of collage on hand-textured surfaces, then paint in response to those visual cues. I use a combination of acrylic and watercolor, applying dozens of layers to create subtle depths in field and color." Venues: Cecile Moochnek, Andrea Schwartz, Fresh Paint Art Advisors.

Kathleen Lack

Novato, CA
www.kathleenlack.com • 415.883.5363

VINTAGE HAT. Oil. 14" x 11"

"When I observe people, I see a soft golden hue against the face, the strength and beauty of a dancer's body, an expression of emotional involvement when playing the cello. These figures and the emotions they evoke are what I am compelled to express."
Venues: Marin Art Festival, Sausalito Art Festival, Lyonshead Gallery.

Margaret Lord

San Rafael, CA
calilord@msn.com • 415.499.8096

SKYRISE VIEW. Polaroid transfer watercolor. 10" x 8"

"I use Polaroid transfers to express the fleeting beauty of everyday scenes. The transfers are diffused and lacy—like memories where, over time, gaps appear and images soften. They reveal a sentimental reflection of life where the most common item or place becomes imbued with a precious quality." Venues: Marin Art Festival, Marin Open Studios.

Jeannie Lydon

Oakland, CA
jeannie@door7gallery.com

PHARE ELECTIQUE. Acrylic on panel. 24" x 32"

"I paint in acrylic and charcoal on panel, inspired by linear city streets, red brick architecture of historical warehouses and the mechanics of pedaling bicyclists. 1958 Fairlanes and stick-shift bicycles are considered our past, although we still enjoy using them today." Venue: Hang Gallery.

Derek Lynch

San Francisco, CA
www.lynchart.com • 415.822.8377

IDE 1. Acrylic on canvas. 50" x 49"

"I compose with natural and man-made elements: botanical, electronic, computer, and mechanical objects. I employ multiple layers of paint and color to invent images that recall the remnants of natural patterns and fractals in a textured, complex composition." Venues: SFMOMA Artists Gallery, Toomey Tourell Gallery, Kathryn Markel Fine Arts.

Debra Maddox

Mill Valley, CA • 415.383.4065
www.deborahmaddoxfineart.com

REFLECTION. Polaroid on watercolor paper with pastels. 24" x 24"

"I use Polaroid manipulation, maneuvering emulsion like oil paint, and sometimes apply pastels or paint to intensify the composition. Each subject is selected to evoke an emotional response, while capturing the relationship of light and shadow, color and texture, and shape and form." Venues: Sausalito Art Festival, Marin Open Studios.

John Maher

Rowena Dell, OR
john@maherart.com • 541.478.0171

ALONG THE BEACH. Photograph. 27" x 32"

"I use vintage photographic techniques to create contemporary art. Hand-coloring my duo-toned, silver gelatin prints allows me to create unique images, each with its own atmosphere—communicating the quality of light and emotional impact of a particular landscape." Venues: Zapature Gallery, Reflections Gallery, Earthworks Gallery.

STUDIO. Oil on canvas. 52" x 48"

"Having traveled and lived in many parts of the world, I incorporate universal aspects of life's strength and perseverance into my work. My paintings are emotional yet serene. Working in layers I achieve unity by harmonizing the contrasts." Venue: Central Studios.

Stela Mandel

Greenbrae, CA
smandel334@aol.com • 415.461.9159

JULIA ON A TRAIN. Oil on canvas. 16" x 20"

"Unlike my medical illustration work, or even my mixed media abstracts, I paint these studies for the pleasure of feeling the paint drive my brush across the canvas. It is almost by coincidence that the paintings resemble what I see." Venue: Marin Open Studios.

David Mark

San Francisco, CA
www.markresourcesusa.com • 415.239.0230

THE SPIRIT OF PLANETARY EXPLORATION. Oil on canvas. 6' x 10'

"My work addresses favorable natural qualities that invited life to prosper in our world, and invoke a larger, rapidly unfolding astrobiological universe. The interaction of penetrated and reflected light elicits a place of moving vistas, where sky and terrain converge."
Venues: SFMOMA Artists Gallery, British Airways Video Installation, SPIE Conference.

CRANE. Oil, gold leaf on paper. 42" x 32"

"Through the metaphor of bird symbols and imagery, I communicate visually. Creation becomes an expression of flight, transcendence and spirit. I become a singer, protector and bird of prey. Birds are mystical creatures, captured in artwork to convey a presence and a journey." Venues: Oakland Museum Collectors Gallery, Shamwari Gallery.

CANOCOTA. Watercolor. 30" x 22"

"The images that attract me and constitute the integrity of my work are those which are linked to man in its daily chores, its surrounding and attitudes—people who unintentionally resist being absorbed by the huge progress of civilization and who fully exercise their humanity." Venues: Settler's West Gallery, Celebration of Fine Art.

GROWING OUT. Oil on canvas. 48" x 36"

"My paintings are based in nature, though not literally so. I begin with a layer of one textured color, then add color, some shapes, lines, or whatever appeals to me. Eventually the result reminds me of, say, wind, night, or galaxy, and I finish the painting to convey that impression." Venues: SFMOMA Artists Gallery, Hang Gallery, Joyce Gordon Gallery.

TRANQUILITY. Encaustic, original photo, panel. 8" x 10"

"I use a variety of media and techniques, including acrylic, ink, oil, photography, and encaustic to discover and define images. I enjoy the cross-pollination and interplay of different processes, allowing the playful and accidental to come forth as they do in nature." Venue: San Francisco Open Studios.

Clem McCarthy

Sausalito, CA
www.clemmccarthy.com • 415.331.1560

TERRA LINDA AUTUMN. Oil on canvas. 24" x 30"

"I have always been fascinated with the off-the-beaten-path places of California, and try to capture their emotional and historical sense in my painting. In a way, these small towns remained locked in the 1950s and '60s, which in these ever-changing times holds a great appeal to me—and hopefully to the viewer." Venues: Marin Open Studios, ICB Shows.

Terry McIlrath

Eugene, OR
joule@efn.org • 541.343.3743

ANTIGENERIC DRIFT. Drawing. 10" x 8"

"My drawings are made with an ink-transfer process, which results in a rich black line and gray tones. The drawings are individually hand-colored with water media. The content depicts schematic images of abstract concepts and familiar symbols."
Venues: Gallery 33, Afflare Arts Gallery, Portland Art Festival.

Masako Miki

Berkeley, CA
www.masakomiki.com • 510.527.9081

CHAMELEON II. Pastel on paper. 16" x 43"

"My work is inspired by the everyday observations of objects, events, and experiences. I intend to suggest the sense of mystery and interrelationships by juxtaposing seemingly unrelated images, marks and patterns. Within the visual vocabulary, I wish to decipher the unknown from the known." Venues: SFMOMA Artists Gallery, Berkeley Open Studios.

James Minden

Portland, OR
jamesminden@comcast.net • 503.292.7914

FOCUS. Acrylic on canvas. 48" x 36"

"My paintings and monotypes are based on the exploration of shapes, lines, texture and color. The abstract, colorful and subtle geometric imagery creates an ambiguous sense of space and movement. I want the images to encourage the viewer to interact with them emotionally, physically and intellectually." Venue: Marghitta Feldman Gallery.

Maralyn Miller

Los Gatos, CA
www.geocities.com/maralynmiller • 408.354.6747

FIELD OF HAYSTACKS. Oil on canvas. 24" x 36"

"For the past few years I have focused my passion for painting on my interpretation of the rolling, golden summer hills of California and the still unpopulated areas. Acrylics and oils are my media." Venues: Voshan Gallery, Valley Art Gallery, Smith Gallery.

Mark & Myshel Morgan

Campbell, CA
www.mmorganphotography.com

KEY LARGO TREE. Colored photograph. 16" x 20"

"We are self-taught artists who have spent years developing our own colorizing techniques, which we combine with traditional photographic processes. Our black and white with subtle color, along with a stylistic perspective, often make it difficult for viewers to accept our images as having been originally seen through a lens."

Barbara Nilsson

Camino, CA
www.barbaranilsson.com • 530.644.5294

UNSAID. Oil on canvas. 16" x 20"

"I work in a variety of media (oil, acrylic, monoprinting and encaustic) and
incorporate a textural feeling that adds to the overall work. When painting I
aspire to capture the moment, the human condition, the texture of life."
Venues: Gallery El Dorado, Camino Hotel, WORKS Gallery.

Paul Ogren

Oakhurst, CA
www.lightscapegallery.net • 559.641.7771

MYSTIC FALLS (Banff National Park). Photograph. 15.5" x 19.5"

"I seek awesome light to make large-format images, both natural and architectural. The landscape images have subtle or rich textures, with a strong three-dimensional quality. Architectural images reflect the character of older structures and the effects of nature." Venues: KPFA Crafts Fair, The Southwest Art Festival.

Sharon Paster

Kentfield, CA
thepasters@earthlink.net • 415.457.8671

MEMORIES OF DAD. Oil on canvas. 48" x 36"

"I want to convey what cannot be seen. Through the layering and scratching of paint in my work, I aim to juxtapose physical reality with the emotions that lie just under the surface." Venues: Marin Open Studios, Magnolia Gallery.

Frank Patt

San Francisco, CA
415.826.2126

THIN PLACES. Oil on canvas. 60" x 48"

"My work consists of layered grounds of oil paint incised with renderings of images, and symbols, revealing surfaces that expose some of my personal and subconscious interactions with the paint. The histories and stories that emerge may be memories from the past, feelings occurring in the present, or emotions yet to be felt." Venue: Hang Art.

Daniel Phill

San Francisco, CA
www.danielphill.com • 415.864.2284

DAVIT. Acrylic on paper. 30" x 44"

"I have been working in a place between composing and dissolving images. These landscape-inspired abstractions come from nature and intuition. Brush painting, primitive art, and abstract expressionism are among the styles of art that inspire my work."
Venues: George Billis Gallery, Karan Ruhlen Gallery, SFMOMA Artists Gallery.

Harold Pickern

San Diego, CA
hpickern@hotmail.com • 619.698.1834

BOYS WITH ROCKS (Diptych). Acrylic on canvas. 30" x 48"

"My subjects speak about the passing of people and the things that they leave behind. In contrast to the current veneer of architecture that we live with, I look for derelicts that resonate with my knowledge and passion. These are almost always found on the periphery." Venues: Sausalito Art Festival, Mill Valley Fall Art Festival, LaQuinta Art Festival.

Steffen Plistermann

Seattle, WA
www.plistermann.com • 206.353.8011

SOLITUDE #3. Oil on canvas. 18" x 24"

"When I paint, my mind is at rest, and while I will go through a range of emotions,
I always experience a feeling of serenity. Regardless of the type of painting I am
working on, it is this feeling of calm and quiet that I want to share with the viewer."
Venues: Serendipity, Zado Gallery, Ryan Gallery.

VANTAGE POINT #7. Mixed media on wood. 15" x 15"

"Whether it is sculpture or painting, I work in series. Once I envision a concept,
I start exploring it, until I feel I have expressed what I wanted to say. I often use
colors to project a mood or a state of being." Venue: Steel Gallery.

Leslie Printis

Foster City, CA
printis@best.com • 650.867.8264

MAN CROSSING STREET. Oil on canvas. 20" x 23"

"My oil paintings are known for use of dramatic light and colors anchored both in the classical and contemporary styles. Art has become a tool to explore the power of color and its history and influences on culture." Venues: Hunters Point Open Studios, San Francisco African American Historical & Cultural Society Museum.

Camille Przewodek

Petaluma, CA
www.przewodek.com • 707.762.4125

GOLDEN GATE CONVERSATION. Oil on canvas. 12" x 16"

"Color that expresses light and atmosphere can make even the most mundane scene strikingly beautiful. I often go back to the same place at different times of day to capture the nuances of different light effects." Venue: Youngman Gallery.

Joe Ramos

San Francisco, CA
ramosart@pacbell.net • 415.386.8659

STONE WARRIOR. Monotype. 30" x 22"

"Coming from a photography background, I make monotypes for the opportunity to express myself visually in a non-objective and unconscious way. The act of making a monotype is almost like play—serendipity has a major role. Monotype themes tend to be about duality and mystery." Venues: Contemporary Crafts Market, SF Open Studios.

Mary Curtis Ratcliff

Berkeley, CA
www.marycurtisratcliff.com • 510.526.8472

TWO BIRDS. Pigmented ink-jet print. 36" x 53"

"I transfer my photographic imagery onto hand-made paper, and further develop the
compositions using graphite, prismacolor, acrylic and collage. Through these images,
I hope to evoke a sense of mystery, open to the layered interplay of memory and
imagination." Venues: SFMOMA Artists Gallery, Copia, Katonah Museum of Art.

Dianne Romaine

San Rafael, CA
maxamp@earthlink.net • 415.492.0965

POLYCHROME #10. Watercolor. 13.5" x 28"

"My work involves simplifying and isolating elements such as line, composition, color, or shape, using an economy of materials. To illuminate these elements, I use a reductive approach. These paintings investigate color relationships, and the density of color."
Venues: SFMOMA Artists Gallery, Linda Fairchild Art, Headlands Center for the Arts.

Jenny Sandbo

Burlington, WA
www.blueorchidart.bizhosting.com • 360.755.0746

NIGHT LANDSCAPE. Pastel, acrylic. 13.5" x 13.5"

"I live in the lush green tranquility of the Pacific Northwest. My love for this landscape is reflected in my painting. I am particularly drawn to the movement and colors of the sky." Venues: Northwest Flower & Garden Show, Bellevue Art Museum Fair, Home Comfort Fine Art & Antiques.

Lori Slater

Cambria, CA
www.lorislater.com • 805.927.4047

POOL AT DUSK. Watercolor. 20.5" x 17"

"I have a penchant for painting objects, whether in a still life, an interior, or garden landscape. Combining shape and symbol with bold, imaginative color, I explore the relationship or dialogue between these objects." Venues: Beverly Hills Art Show, Marin Fall Art Festival, Bronze, Silver & Gold Gallery.

Steve Solinsky

Nevada City, CA
www.solinksyphoto.com • 530.265.5977

MYTHIC LIGHT (Tuscany). Photograph. 18" x 23"

"My images record fascination—a quiet moment of awe, where the dance of light and shadow transform the familiar world into the magnificent or mysterious. A printmaker for decades, my rendering of the negative defines the expression of the photographic print.' Venues: Portland Arts Festival, Kings Mountain Art Festival, Mill Valley Fall Art Festival.

Glenn Steiner

Fairfax, CA
www.glennsteiner.com • 415.459.2001

STEFANI'S TOES (Garapata Beach, CA). Silver gelatin print. 9.5" x 6.4"

"Despite modern man's best attempts to distinguish himself from nature, the human form and a rock, to me, are similar parts of the larger whole. The nude is a rock. The model becomes another fantastic form in an unreal, beautiful landscape. The two are equal, balanced, inseparable." Venue: SFMOMA Artists Gallery.

Ann Switzer

Larkspur, CA
www.annswitzer.com • 415.927.9003

MONTECITO GOLD. Watercolor. 9" x 12"

"The visual richness of nature continues to be my inspiration. Using traditional watercolor techniques, I focus on the dramatic effects of light on color and form. I hope to inspire the viewer to look at nature with an increased appreciation and sense of wonder."
Venues: Art Works Downtown, Marin Open Studios.

Elizabeth Tocher

Pacifica, CA
650.359.6624

ABSTRACT WITH RUNNING FIGURE. Acrylic. 20.5" x 13.25"

"My paintings, for the most part, are semi-abstract. I much enjoy the challenge of combining geometric shapes, architectural elements and images from nature to develop the most interesting relationship of these components as I can and, in doing so, I hope to engage the imagination of all viewers." Venue: Sanchez Art Center.

Ann Curran Turner

Sausalito, CA
415.331.5126

THE LAST AFFAIR. Oil on canvas. 24" x 18"

"I am drawn to the human figure, fascinated by people and their unending complexities. I am driven to capture their elegance, ornamentation, humor, fragility, absurdity—the common vulnerability of our skin, guts, hearts—but most importantly—their attitude, spirit, energy, and life force."

Brett Varney

Bellingham, WA
www.brettvarney.com • 360.671.9026

ISLAND MEADOW. Oil, pastel. 14" x 14"

"I am fascinated by the ability of color, line, and texture to convey emotion. Use of black outlines intensifies my work without interfering with the psychological effect of my color palette. Drawing energizes me, and I want the viewer to experience that energy." Venues: Portland Arts Festival, Best of the Northwest, Kings Mountain Art Festival.

Edward Vliek

Eugene, OR
541.343.7163

VERNAZZA TWILIGHT. Silver bromide photograph. 16" x 20"

"As a black and white photographer of thirty years, I have found a unique quality of light—a luminous aura which visual artists treasure. I find this light in Italy and the Oregon dunes. Photographing these areas, all my senses open." Venues: Best of the Northwest, Portland Rose Festival, Art in the Vineyard.

Wendy Willis

Phoenix, AZ
wswillis@yahoo.com • 602.750.3845

OUT OF THE DEPTHS. Reduction relief print. 9" x 12"

"I love the immediacy of monoprinting and the complexity of reductive relief printing. My subjects are primarily family, oceans and swimming pools. Since I was little, I lived underwater in the pool on family vacations. In my 'Swimmer' series, I am enjoying the pleasures I find in the pool and exploring my inner spaces." Venue: Arizona Print Group.

Beverly Wilson

Napa, CA
www.beverlywilson.com • 707.253.9247

HILLSIDE HARVEST. Oil on canvas. 40" x 30"

"I am inspired to paint the beauty and simplicity of everyday life. The land and man's place in it are my favorite themes. With a unique palette of colors and bold compositions, I strive to turn an ordinary moment into the extraordinary by expressing it with vibrant energy." Venues: Art on Main Gallery, Sausalito Art Festival.

Karyn Young

Fairfax, CA
www.karynyoung.com • 415.454.0389

BAMBOO GARDEN. Mixed media on paper. 24" x 36"

"I celebrate the momentary, welcoming its influence wherever and whenever its source,
with a visual style reflecting fourteen years of immersion in Japanese tradition and culture.
Moving across time, using mixed media and collage, I present the familiar in a new light."
Venues: Verne Collection, Institute for Health and Healing, Tiburon Fine Arts.

TREE OF LIFE. Porcelain, oak base. 18" x 16" x 7"

"My passion for this fluid medium has not diminished throughout my many years of working with clay, a fundamental earth substance. To take a chunk of porcelain and turn it into an illuminating piece of artful beauty is my joy." Venues: Fusion Gallery, Green Mountain Studios.

Dawn Barnett

San Rafael, CA
www.dabarstudio.com

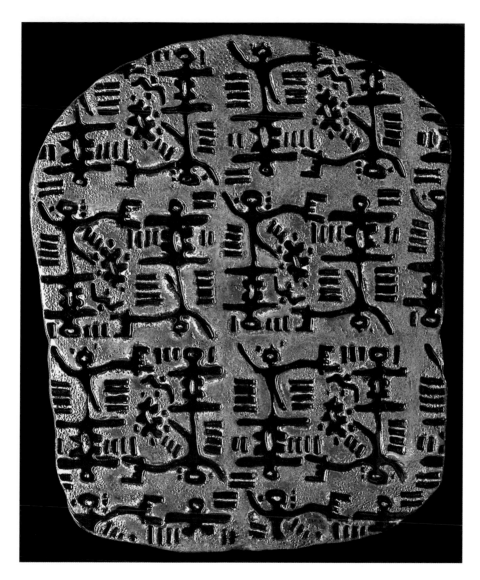

LOVE IN BLOODY FLOW. Ceramic. 18" x 15"

"Compelling carvings incorporated onto clay sculpture is the basis of my art. Study in Italy and extensive traveling have enhanced my interpretation of major life events and the deaf culture." Venues: Marin Open Studios, San Rafael Lagoon Festival, Celebration of Craftswomen.

IDLY WILD. Pit fired ceramic. 24" h

"My pieces deal with layers of time and space, the power of the soul to endure throughout the ages, to struggle, to grow and to transcend. My passion lies in the process, the creation of the work, the new and unrevealed ideas, and the unpredictability of pit-firing."

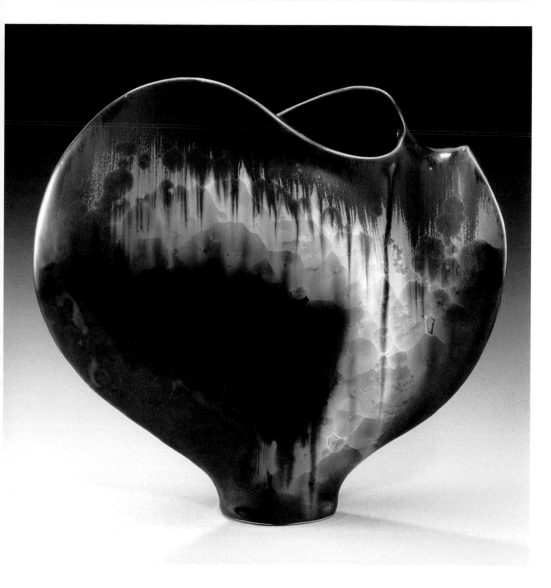

SANDSTORM ENVELOPE VASE. Porcelain. 11" x 11" x 3"

"My pieces exhibit my ongoing interest in form—sculpting porcelain into out-of-round shapes that are organic, sometimes almost figurative. I spray layers of glazes to accentuate the curves, shadows and mood of each piece." Venues: Seattle Art Museum Gallery, Earthworks Galleries, Bellevue Art Museum Fair.

PAINTING OF 3 VASES WITH FLOWERS. Acrylic, porcelain, paper flowers. 40" x 28"

"I create functional wall vases in different shapes and styles, and have
been experimenting with—and teaching workshops in—printing techniques
for colored porcelains that allow surfaces with more depth and detail."
Venues: ACGA Festivals, ACC San Francisco, SF Flower and Garden Show.

Rachel Deist

San Francisco, CA
clayfriend@aol.com • 415.819.9198

UNTITLED. Ceramic. 6" x 4.5"

"Achieving balance between ceramic form and crystalline glaze is a challenge in my work. Classic Asian vessels and Southeast Asian temples inspire me. I see nature both in the glaze, with its geologic echoes, and in form, where undulating shapes suggest the feminine." Venues: SF Open Studios, Verdigris Gallery, Art Fusion Winter Show.

Jeff Downing

San Rafael, CA
jdowning@sfsu.edu • 415.499.8105

TAMALE. Ceramic. 16" x 13" x 11"

"My work with dog imagery seeks to invoke feelings concerning our relationship with the natural world. Studying the dog—with all of its expressiveness, intelligence and sensitivity —I hope to lead us to a better understanding of the connection between culture and nature." Venues: John Natsoulas Gallery, Tercera Gallery, NaPua Gallery.

Susan Duhan Felix

Berkeley, CA
sdfelix@aol.com • 510.841.1781

PUTTING TOGETHER THE PIECES. Ceramic. 24" x 9" x 2.5"

"My pit-fired work attempts to integrate darkness and light. This process cannot be forced.
It involves faith in creative patience, the unconscious, and the world's inherent goodness.
At times my labor is shattered, then a new shape reveals itself from the broken pieces."
Venues: The Skirball Museum Shop, The Judah Magnes Museum Shop, ACGA Palo Alto.

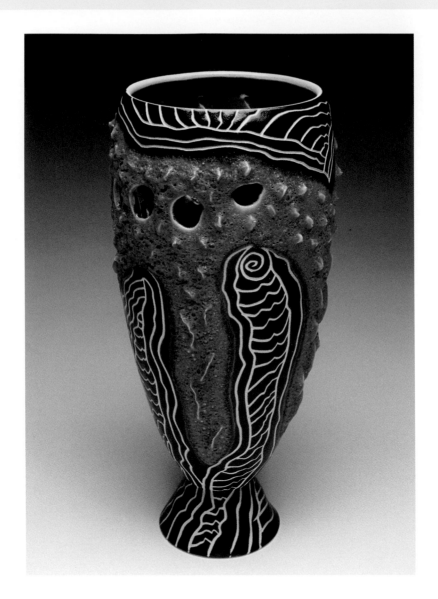

RIBCAGE VESSEL. Ceramic. 10" h

"Clay absorbs and reflects what is going on for me, allows me to see how I am feeling. By combining texture, applied bumps, cut out windows and the graphic quality of sgraffito, I turn ideas into forms that are a link to my inner landscape." Venues: ACGA Festivals, ACC San Francisco and Baltimore, Exploding Head Gallery, Celebration of Craftswomen.

Alison Gooding

Seattle, WA
www.beadpoles.com • 206.937.6537

BEAD POLES (installation detail). Ceramic.

"Bead Poles—sculptural adornment for any environment. Initially designed to add color and height to a garden, these ceramic sculptures have evolved into complex pieces of art that combine handmade beads of varying sizes, textures, shapes and colors. The beauty of this process is that the creative possibilities are unlimited."

Jane B. Grimm

San Francisco, CA
www.janebgrimm.com • 415.922.2823

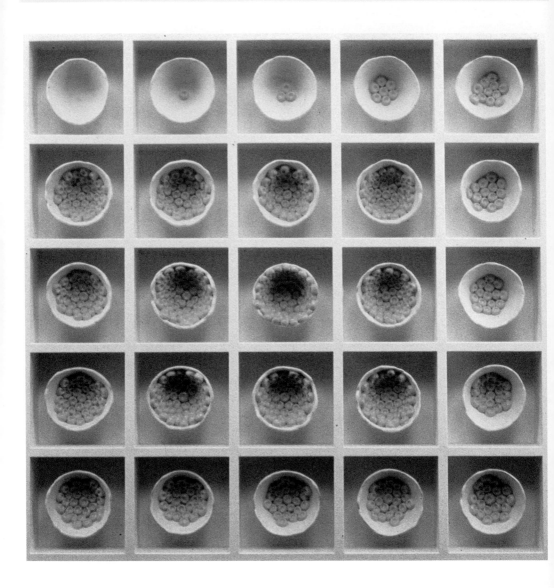

VORTEX IV. Ceramic, wood. 28" x 28" x 3"

"My ceramic sculptures concentrate on the study of forms and the effects that light, shadow and space have on an object. The repetitious use of an image accentuates its importance. Color is used to enhance the subtleties of the variations and alterations of a form." Venues: ACGA Shows, Richmond Art Center, Oakland Museum Sculpture Court.

ENLIGHTENMENT. Ceramic stoneware. 21" x 19" x 8"

"My sculptures talk about journeys, pilgrimages and cycles. They represent a journey through time and places. My pieces have a spiritual and mystical quality. They often have a stone-like and pre-historic feeling to them. I combine the permanence and heaviness of history with the fragile evolution within each person."

Trudi Klinger

Hood River, OR
mysticmudstudio@aol.com • 541.354.1238

HARLEQUIN HARVEST. Ceramic. 18" d

"My pottery celebrates the bountiful fruit orchards surrounding my Hood River Valley studio. I appreciate the simple perfection and beauty of each shape of fruit I render. Juxtaposing classic geometric patterns with playful, organic images adds vibrancy and dimension." Venues: Bellevue Art Museum Fair, Fireworks Gallery, Salem Art Festival.

Antonia Lawson

San Rafael, CA
www.silverhawk5.com/lawson • 415.507.9909

THREE PARTY ANIMALS. Ceramic. 24" x 8" each

"I am a British, Hong Kong-born ceramic sculptor. My work spans from whimsical anthropomorphic animals and political genre to organic pods and functional planters. My pieces are hand-crafted and often presented in a series." Venues: John Natsoulas Gallery, The Museum of Craft and Folk Art, ACGA Palo Alto and San Francisco.

Shirl Lipkin

Warren, OR
503.366.5661

FIELD-RUN SERIES: SIPPING CUPS & TRAY. Ceramic. 17" x 10" x 5"

"I spend each spring and fall atop a roaring tractor, working grain fields. Over and over the earth opens and closes, the marks and patterns a silent code, revealing stories of what was and what will come to be. These are the marks that adorn the surfaces of my pots; each piece a story from the earth." Venues: ACC Shows, Portland Ceramic Show, Portland Arts Fest.

Marilyn MacKenzie

Capitola, CA
831.688.6546

FISH ON SPHERES. Terracotta. 27" x 12" x 8"

"My work is designed as ornamentation for home, garden, and public spaces.
Many pieces combine animal forms, familiar ceramic styles, and strategically
placed geometric accents. Often the work is designed to interact with water."
Venue: ACC San Francisco.

Paddy McNeely

Seattle, WA
206.723.5153

BLACK WILLOW. Ceramic. 31" h

"I specialize in functional porcelain with matte black glaze developed to enhance the simplicity evident in the work. Components often include dyed English willow and black bamboo. My work is influenced by pottery of ancient Japan and Korea." Venues: The Bellevue Art Museum Fair, Northwest Craft Center, Fire's Eye.

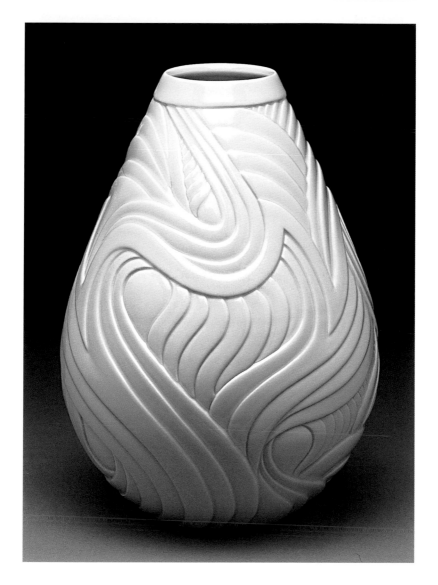

TEMPEST. Carved porcelain. 14" x 9" x 9"

"I am inspired by the symmetry and dynamic surfaces of the pottery of Mata Ortiz in Central Mexico, and the sensuality of the Art Nouveau movement. I love the juxtaposition of the cold, still surface of the porcelain and the organic movement that I try to create in the carving." Venues: Bellagio, Alabaster, Sausalito Art Festival.

Reiko Miyagi

Vallejo, CA
707.552.7264

GARDEN TEAPOT. Ceramic. 6" x 12.5"

"My work is inspired by shapes from nature and my belief in the connectedness of all beings and objects. I greatly enjoy seeing my work used to help celebrate life's daily rituals or to make harmonious surroundings, both of which sustain a good spirit."
Venues: ACCI Gallery, Mill Valley Fall Art Festival, ACGA Festivals.

Jeff Morales

McKinleyville, CA
morales1191@cox.net • 707.839.2168

SATURN JAR. Ceramic. 11" x 14"

"I have always focused on design, and been most influenced by forms emanating from the arts and crafts movement, such as Mission and Bungalow styles. These design elements, emphasizing detail and craftsmanship, are the principles guiding my efforts." Venues: ACGA Festivals, Kings Mountain Art Festival, Art in the Pearl.

Kathy Pallie

San Rafael, CA
kpallie@comcast.net • 415.485.5797

TROPICAL TWIST. Low-fire clay, wire, glazes. 40" x 12"

"With nature as my inspiration, I delve into the functional, structural, colorful and multidimensional capabilities of clay. My passion for flowers, the water world, and the outdoors is expressed in styles ranging from brightly-colored, whimsical artworks to more organic, earth-toned, tactile sculptures." Venue: Marin Society of Artists.

Christina Pearce

San Diego, CA
www.christinapearce.com • 619.701.1683

PROMETHIUM. Ceramic. 10" x 17" x 14.25"

"Movement and optical effects are significant elements in my work. The importance
of these rudiments has emerged from an investigation into the dynamics of visual
perception and the ways in which one's understanding of an object can be challenged."
Venues: Art and Cultural Center, Cannon Art Center, Kellogg University Art Gallery.

Bob Pool

Berkeley, CA
bpoolpottery@attbi.com

COLLARED VASES. Ceramic stoneware. 16" h, 24" h

"I am inspired by Asian and African motifs, particularly as expressed in fabrics. I often emphasize the pot's surface, as if the piece was suspended in space. I seek an interesting form enhanced by rich colors and patterns." Venues: Left Bank Gallery, Q Street Gallery, Appalachian Spring.

Rachel Porter

Sebastopol, CA
415.824.1684

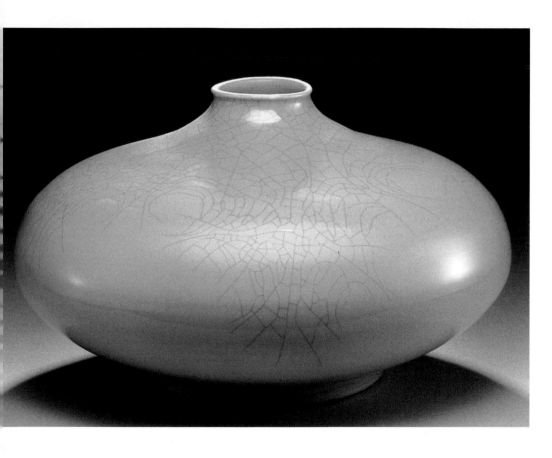

YELLOW ORB. Porcelain. 12" x 16" x 16"

"I create simple forms of beauty. For me, working in porcelain is a metaphor for life. Porcelain is fragile, offering relentless technical challenges which only enhance its beauty and allure. My glazes are formulated to capture the spontaneity of life and the rich tradition of ancient porcelain." Venues: ACGA Palo Alto, ARTrails Open Studios.

VASES. Ceramic. 12" h

"We, like all potters, deal in the art of transformation. It is what keeps us coming back—putting together the familiar to form the new." Venues: Freehand, Guild.com, ACC San Francisco, ACGA Palo Alto.

PEACH URN. Ceramic. 8" x 14"

"My work reflects the natural world. Current designs explore fruits, vegetables and flowers in rich, vibrant colors. I enjoy the rituals that surround mealtime. My pots are an effort to extend that joyful experience to others. All are handmade, handpainted, and completely functional." Venues: The Real Mother Goose Gallery, Plaza Design.

Rosanne Reynolds

Oakland, CA
rreynolds.snarkboojum.com • 510.910.3353

FOUR-AND-TWENTY BLACK BIRDS (detail). Cast gypsum. 24 at 12" x 4" each

"My sculpture explores commonalities within the human condition—the implications of loss, choice, and memory. Using various materials, I create detailed and multi-layered narrative, employing gestural beauty and intricate surfaces as both lure and reward for the strong emotional content of the work." Venues: San Jose State Univ., CCACA Davis.

Inge Roberts

Whidbey Island, WA
ingejohn@whidbey.com • 360.730.1168

TERRA SIGILLATA. Porcelain. 9" x 10" x 8"

"To work with clay is to work on shunning all but a few of its temptations. I focus on the translucency of porcelain. I explore and expose its raw softness. I rip, imprint and layer the mud with found and invented images. Even when words dominate a piece, I record but send no message." Venues: V. Breier Gallery, ACGA Shows, Wild Lily Tea Room.

Jan Schachter

Portola Valley, CA
www.janschachter.com • 650.851.3754

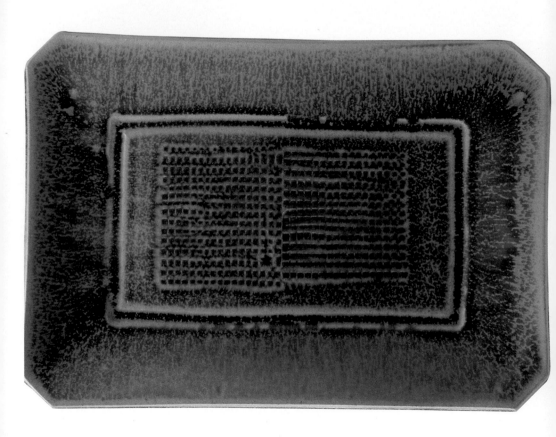

SLAB PLATE. Stoneware. 11" x 15.5" x 1.25"

"I enjoy making pots for everyday use. I constantly search for the perfect surface
and ideal shape while striving to create pots that have life and vitality."
Venues: ACGA Festivals, Silicon Valley Open Studios, V. Breier Gallery.

AMPHORA VESSEL. Stoneware. 10" x 6" x 6"

"My vessels are heavily influenced by pre-Columbian and Asian cultures. Each stoneware vessel is thrown on the potter's wheel, then indented by eye and hand using custom steel- tipped tools. A red iron oxide wash is applied to the recesses of the exterior, then the excess is wiped away." Venues: ACC San Francisco and Baltimore.

ABSTRACT RAVEN PLATTER. Ceramic. 27" d

"The potters wheel and the paint brush are our vehicles through an intuitive landscape of ethnic design and ancient form. We utilize the raw clay juxtaposed with satin glaze surfaces to explore the endless interplay of texture and color and hope our work echoes of the past." Venues: Worthington Gallery, Chambers Gallery, Clay Hands Gallery.

SPLIT VASE WITH BLACK DAMSEL FLY. Porcelain. 14" h

"Our collaborative art reflects twenty-five years of shared interests—from Chris's zoological pursuits to Jan's love of richly glazed surfaces and classic forms. The challenge has been to combine these interests into a cohesive body of work."
Venues: ACGA Palo Alto and San Francisco, Highlight Gallery.

Joan Bazaz

Seattle, WA
www.bazazglass.com • 206.783.8090

LAMP. Glass. 9" x 7" x 4"

"Even before asking questions about my patterns or technique, people hold my glass pieces up to the light. Whether making jewelry, tableware, window panels, custom lighting or glass sculpture, my main fascination is with subtle shifts in color and texture occurring as light changes." Venues: Museum of Glass, Bellevue Art Museum Fair.

Rebecca Bergsma

Monroe, WA
www.rebeccabergsma.com • 425.788.1238

WALL SCULPTURE. Glass. 30" x 30"

"After more than twenty-five years as a stained glass artist, I discovered a whole new world of potential using the ancient process of heating glass to fusion temperatures. I use cut and layered glass heated to varying temperatures, and techniques such as sandblasting and metal inclusions." Venue: Rest of the Best Fair.

Rusty Cantor

Berkeley, CA
rustycan@sbcglobal.net • 510.845.6258

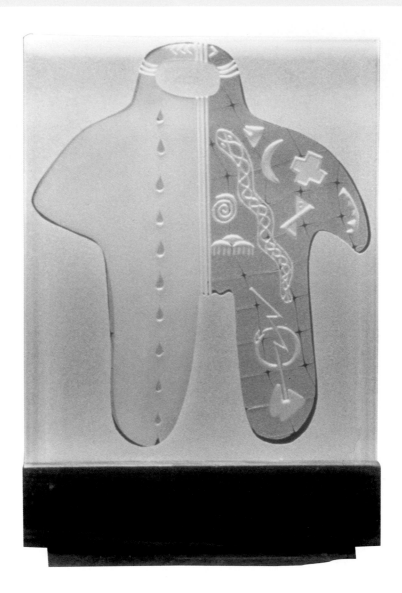

WOMAN WARRIOR. Three layers of glass. 11" x 7"

"The 'Woman Warrior' is a symbol for all women. Rather than go into battle in a conventional sense, she fights against poverty, prejudice, abuse, sexism, racism, ageism, etc. with integrity, courage and spirit—to overcome problems, protect loved ones and improve the world. I use symbols to touch emotions beyond the reach of words."

Eloise Cotton

Martinez, CA
eloisecotton@aol.com • 925.229.1989

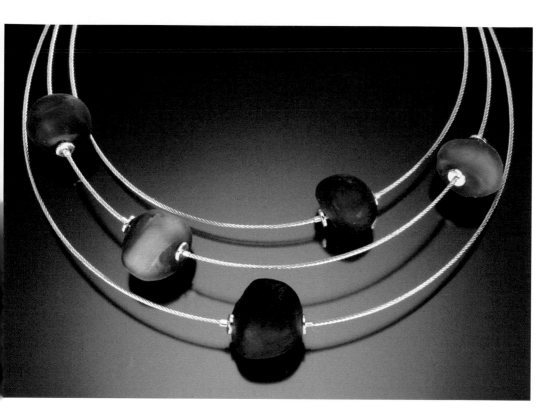

ODD BALL NECKLACE. Glass, wire. 24"

"As a self-taught flameworker, I had freedom to break the rules. My hollow baroque beads result from experiments in odd shapes, and are fabricated to make each one unique. My jewelry designs reflect my fascination with the aesthetics of asymmetry and balance." Venues: V. Breier Gallery, Zosaku, Studio 41.

Steve Ferrera

Berkeley, CA
www.scferrera.com • 510.527.9081

PARASITE SERIES #2. Glass, ceramic, bronze. 6" x 19" x 11"

"My work frequently comments on our evolution as a species, and our de-evolution as hominids, as technology and progress slowly make our opposable thumbs obsolete."
Venues: Bay Area Glass Institute, Triton Museum, Berkeley Open Studios.

RUTILE. Sculpted glass. 33" x 17" x 4"

"By elaborating on the fluidity of glass, I interpret nature through this material, creating unique shapes and 'environmental skins' for my art. 'Rutile' is inspired by nature's movements—flowing water and fire. Its transparency and color help to express these elements through its form." Venues: ACC Shows, Buyers Market of America.

GRACE. Kiln-cast crystal. 12" x 10" x 2.5"

"Utilizing texture, form and light, I explore the balance from physical to spiritual in glass sculpture and *giclée* prints. Sensual photographs of macro patterns of sand, water, grass and other natural elements carry on a dialogue with the minimal glass sculptures."
Venues: Andora Gallery, Sandra Ainsley Gallery, Starfish Gallery.

Dan & Eve King-Lehman

Gaya Glass • Somis, CA
www.gayaglass.com • 805.386.4069

DESERT RIM PLATTER. Glass. 18" x 18"

"We create functional and decorative glass artworks that ride the line between applicability and art." Venues: ACC San Francisco, Contemporary Craft Market, ACGA San Francisco and Palo Alto, The White House Permanent Collection.

Tim Lindemann

Santa Barbara, CA
805.252.1810

BIRTH OF A PLANET. Glass. 17" h

"Glass is a versatile medium that enables me to make color and form combinations directly from imagination. I prefer not to use obvious symbolism, but use shapes and color combinations that evoke an emotion. I am also strongly influenced by the aesthetics of nature." Venues: Dovetail Collection, Carlyn Gallery, Sausalito Art Festival.

David Lindsay

Benicia, CA
www.lindsayartglass.com • 707.748.1336

OLYMPIC BOWL. Blown glass. 12.5" x 13"

"Creating beauty out of fire is what being a glassblower is all about. Working with this hot, fiery liquid is exciting and provides me with instant results. I have been creating glass jewels for over twenty-seven years, and enjoy glass making's fast-paced dance with fire."
Venues: Lindsay Art Glass Gallery, ACGA San Francisco and Palo Alto.

Jeremy Newman

Twisp River Glassworks • Twisp, WA
www.twispriverglass.com • 509.997.2120

BANDED VESSELS. Blown glass. 16" x 8" x 3.3", 13" x 7" x 2.5"

"In my glasswork, I try to express the beauty I see in the natural world. I find inspiration in nature's random textures, unique forms and calming color palette. I bring these elements into my work out of a desire to reconnect people with their roots in nature." Venues: American Museum of Art and Design, Racine Art Museum, LeKae Gallery.

BUBBLE INCALMO CYLINDERS & OVAL VASE. Blown glass. 19" x 6" x 6", 18" x 10" x 5"

"We have designed many series of works using numerous techniques of color and pattern application applied to the surface, creating images relating to the vessel and its form. These images are often encased between layers of clear glass, blown out and stretched, creating a painterly effect." Venues: Gumps, Concepts Gallery, Art & All That Jazz.

Kim Webster

Oakland, CA
www.kwebsterglass.com

NOW THAT'S A GLASS SLIPPER! Blown & hot-worked glass. 18" x 12" x 4"

"Glass has a long history of preserving that which is precious. I work with blown glass and enamels to preserve and share moments in the garden, laughter among friends and memories of people, times and places." Venues: Glass Artist Gallery, Oakland Museum Collectors Gallery, East Bay Open Studios.

Ruby Bettencourt

Lafayette, CA
sacredgems@yahoo.com • 925.934.6362

CYBELE. 18k gold, diamonds, sapphires, pearls. 1.5" x 1"

"Shape, color, texture, and form in the natural world are reflected in my organic approach to fine metal. My unique palette of color draws from my fine arts background. Inspired by sacred traditions of different cultures, my jewelry reflects these in a timeless manner." Venues: Concepts Gallery, Deva, Topeo Gallery.

Dana Driver

Albion, CA
drocks@mcn.org • 707.937.4062

WATER LILY. Pin/pendant. Beachstone with fine silver inlay, sterling silver, 14k gold.

"I collect common beach stones, then carve, texture and inlay them with fine silver and 22k gold. These enhanced stones are the foundation of my work. Since no two stones are exactly alike, all my pieces are unique, fabricated works of wearable art."
Venues: ACC Baltimore & San Francisco, William Zimmer Gallery, Bellagio.

NECKLACE. Silver, glass, ceramic, mother of pearl, beach pebble. 18"

"I find special objects, such as beach and bottle glass with hints of writing or design, then carefully cut them into specific shapes to resemble gemstones worn by time. I want to stimulate the feeling that wearers are enjoying something both modern and ancient."
Venues: Gallery of Jewels, Zosaku Berkeley.

Cornelia Goldsmith

Sausalito, CA
415.332.0802

CROWN RING. 18k gold, diamonds, rubies, sapphires.

"Through my jewelry designs, I strive to capture, with elegance and simplicity, the preciousness of life and its unpredictable flow. The techniques I use are merely tools, the means to get my message across—to inspire the wearer and to touch the soul." Venues: Sausalito Art Festival, ACC San Francisco and St. Paul.

Nancy Goodenough

Monte Rio, CA
nancygoodenough@aol.com

SATURN BRACELET. Dichroic glass, sterling silver.

"To capture the affinity between nature and technology, I frequent hardware stores for inspiration and create art under the redwoods. My signature glass kilnwork is designed to evoke the mystery of tidepools and connectivity with the heavens."
Venues: Buyers Market of American Craft, Best Bead Show, Bead & Button Show.

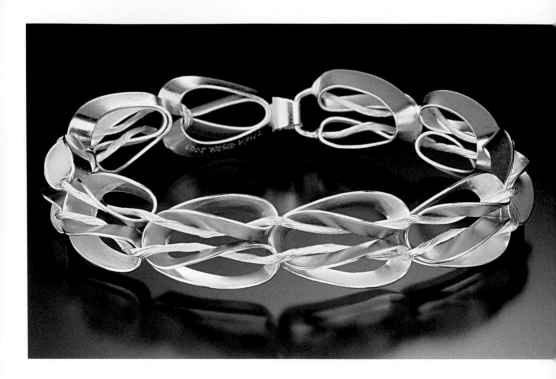

ANGELINE BRACELET. 22k gold & sterling silver bi-metal.

"My work represents a convergence of geometric and organic shapes translated to ornament. Symmetry, pattern repetition and illusions created by contrast fuel my inspiration—to create wearable sculpture which compliments the body and inspires the holder to interpret meaning." Venues: SFMOMA Store, Gallery of Jewels, De Novo.

Ling-Yen Jones

Point Arena, CA
www.ling-yendesigns.com • 707.884.9536

THREE SWALLOWS. Necklace. Sterling silver, blue chalcedony, pearls.

"I define jewelry as creations which are useful, symbolic, identifying, and express personal ideas. My pieces with Asian-like faces are inspired by the feminine, graceful and romantic scenes of the Ukiyo-E period of Japanese art." Venues: Gallery of Jewels, William Zimmer Gallery, V. Breier Gallery.

SUMMER ESSENCE. Sterling silver, coral, turquoise. 28" x 1.5"

"We strive to create thought-provoking sterling silver metalwork designs that embrace
the beauty of nature to offer stunning wearable art. Vinosus is a new attitude
of wearable art—industrial, sophisticated, organic, and refined." Venues:
Seattle Gift Show, Buyers Market of American Craft, Bellevue Art Museum Fair.

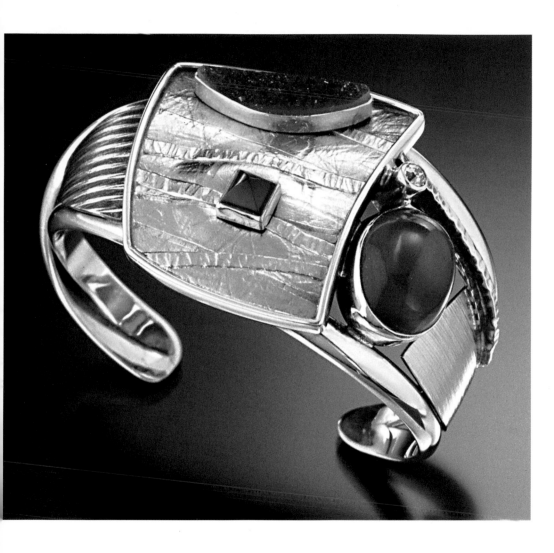

CUFF BRACELET #7. Sterling silver, 22k gold, hessonite, garnet, drusy, agate.

"My work resembles a quilt. I focus on developing patterns, surface textures, and their combinations. Stripes bring rhythm into a piece—swing and attitude. Embossed, high relief areas contrast with softly imprinted ones." Venues: Sausalito Art Festival, Ann Arbor Art Festival, ACC Baltimore.

Kathleen Lamberti

Los Angeles, CA
kathleenlamberti@earthlink.net

POD NECKLACE. Sterling silver, silk. 24"

"My background is in metals, but I couldn't achieve everything I wanted, and found that incorporating fabric has given softness to the metal and allowed me to work with color as well. I have learned to take techniques from each discipline and apply them to the other material." Venues: ACC San Francisco, Sculpture to Wear.

Marcia Macdonald

Eugene, OR
mammetal@prodigy.net • 541.345.7808

STRIPED BROOCH WITH BRUSH. Wood, paint, sterling silver, brush. 4" x 1" x 1.25"

"Most of my pieces are narrative while others express a gesture or form inspired from nature. I create objects to express how divine impulses coexist with earthbound ones, and how serious moments also contain humor." Venues: Velvet da Vinci Gallery, Hibberd/McGrath Gallery.

Louise McGuinness

Oakland, CA
lmcgth@aol.com • 510.547.7636

SEA GARDEN BROOCH. Sterling silver, 18k gold. 3" x 2"

"I explore line and form to make jewelry with the fluidity of a drawing—jewelry that exhibits volume, movement and playfulness. Pieces are fabricated using silver and a variety of karat golds." Venues: Contemporary Crafts Market San Francisco and Santa Monica, Art Baltimore.

REVERSIBLE PEARL NECKLACE. 18k yellow/white gold, freshwater pearls. 17.25"

"High karat gold and platinum interwoven with fine gemstones and rare pearls, are
my artistic focus. European trained, I strive to create minimalist, but striking pieces
combining century-old techniques of fabrication and modern casting processes."
Venues: La Jolla Festival of the Arts, Indian Wells Arts Festival, Kings Mountain Art Fair.

THREE RINGS. Sea glass, 14k gold, sterling silver.

"I collect glass from beaches along the Pacific Coast, always selected with jewelry in mind. The pieces are set in fine silver, sterling silver, or 14K gold. The shape of the glass often decides whether it becomes a necklace, a pair of earrings, or a ring."
Venues: The Artful Eye, KPFA Craft Show, Contemporary Crafts Market.

Kris Borchardt

San Francisco, CA
www.kbsculpture.com • 415.586.1276

THE BLUE MARBLE. Pewter, coated steel, found objects. 52" x 17" x 19"

"The marrow of my work is refuse and found objects. One or two objects inspire the spirit and skeleton, and I connect disparate pieces intuitively. I am currently preoccupied with balance, and with creating simple beauty or meaning from what others leave behind."
Venues: San Francisco Open Studios, Lafayette Art Gallery, A New Leaf Gallery.

WALLPIECE 03.13. Fabricated and patinaed brass. 21" x 27"

"In designing wall pieces, I aim for a balance of form, color, and texture within asymmetric compositions. I fabricate parts for each piece from brass sheet, color them with sculptural patinas, then hammer, etch or grind to create surface texture. Custom work is welcome." Venues: ACC San Francisco, Dunn Mehler Gallery, The Gardener.

Lesley Cantor-Fallihee

Oakland, CA
www.seriouswhimsy.com • 510.339.3412

RECEIVING VESSEL. Steel wire, glass beads. 18" x 16" x 12"

"My joy is weaving and welding organic forms of steel and wire. I often embellish these pieces with glass and metal beads. Beads can communicate a great sense of history and world-wide ethnicity along with their beauty and light."
Venues: ACC San Francisco and Baltimore, V. Breier Gallery, Iota Gallery.

Michael Gard

San Francisco, CA
www.michaelgard.com • 415.933.8153

LEAP. Brass wire. 30" x 28"

"The human figure is a most expressive form. The pose communicates mood, intention, and feeling. Most of my sculptures are mobiles, featuring one or more figures. My work draws on classical sculpture, yet the technique is my own." Venues: ACC San Francisco and Baltimore, Sausalito Art Festival, Ann Arbor Art Festival.

WATERFALL. Cut & bent steel, powder-coat rust finish. 46" x 21, 30" x 33"

"I enjoy metal's tactile appeal, and strive not to distract from its intrinsic beauty. I use movement, shapes, repetitive forms and tactility to explore the familiar and the unknown, and to meld function with beauty and humor." Venues: Bainbridge Arts and Crafts, BKB & Company, Bellevue Art Museum Fair.

VASE 09B. Silicon bronze, cupric patina, gold patina. 19" x 6"

"In a society increasingly disconnected from nature, I hope my vases honor the life that inhabits them and draw attention to the true beauty of some of nature's simpler elements, such as an elegant branch or flowing strands of grass." Venues: Sausalito Art Festival, ACC San Francisco and Baltimore, Dunn Mehler Gallery.

PATINATED BRONZE. Cast from Wasa crispbread, saltine crackers, pasta. 4" x 5" x 2"

"My mother always told me not to play with my food, but I never listened. All
my bronzes are lost-wax cast directly from the food, then painted or patinated."
Venues: ACC San Francisco, V. Breier Gallery.

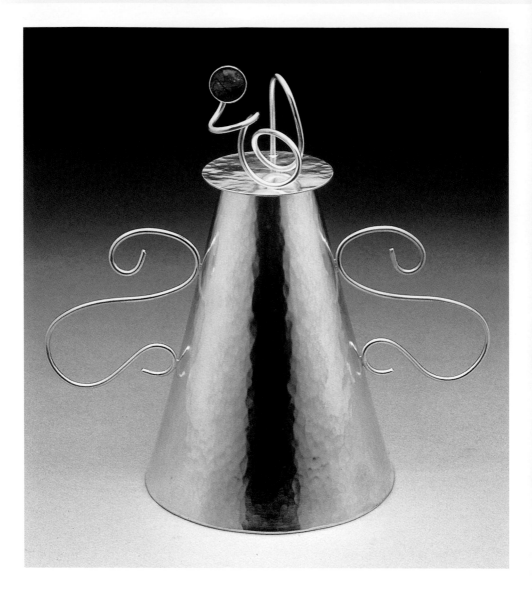

BOTTLED SPIRIT II. Sterling silver, rutialated quartz. 6" x 6" x 4"

"I collect shapes—in my sketchbook, in photos on my workbench, in my memory. Sometimes I begin a piece with one of these forms, sometimes I start with the concept. I work with the form, change its balance, give it movement, and give it life." Venues: ACC San Francisco, V. Breier Gallery.

Lisa Slovis

San Diego, CA
www.lisaslovis.com • 858.490.1336

META-MENORAH. Pewter, bronze. 4" h

"My work includes jewelry, Judaica, and objects for the home. While keeping a serious look by using clean lines, ergonomic forms and a soft whimsical texture, I draw the viewer in, to interact with them on a more intimate and tactile level." Venues: Cherry Creek Arts Festival, ACC San Francisco and Baltimore, Telluride Gallery.

Carmen Valdes

Seattle, WA
www.carmenvaldes.com • 206.523.3427

TIC, TIC, TIC (ring). Sterling silver, rubber. 1" x 1" x 1"

"My aim is simplicity and the beauty therein. I work with clean lines and plain, bold shapes. Many of my designs are of silver and rubber. Together, the materials become inseparable opposites, each defining the other—light and dark, hard and soft, precious and industrial." Venues: ACC San Francisco and Baltimore, CraftBoston.

C. Greg Wilbur

Portland, OR
gswilbur@aol.com • 503.236.1594

LICHEN. Raised bronze. 9" x 7" x 7"

"I raise (hand hammer/squish) form from single sheets of metal. I look to the natural world and the body to find this form. The use of 'one' piece of metal has been my way, making the works very Zen-y." Venues: Velvet da Vinci, Contemporary Crafts Museum and Gallery, ACC San Francisco.

Carol Durham

San Rafael, CA
415.479.4630

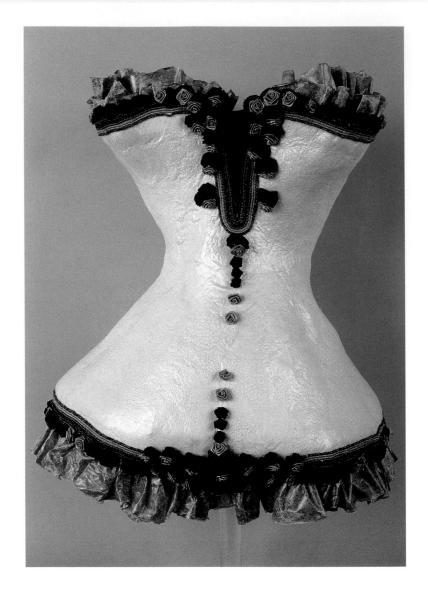

FIFEE LAREE. Gut, beads, silk florals. 24" x 10" x 1"

"I use gut (hog casings) to form art I see as life metaphors. To prepare the gut, I wash it, feed it onto a dowel, cut and split, cut again into workable lengths, and multi-layer over forms. The material is then left to dry. Later the works are often painted or embellished to create the final image." Venues: Artworksdowntown.org, FiberScene.com

Julie Hirota

Roseville, CA
julie@jhiro.com • 916.782.2917

SHAPES AND SIZES. Cloth. 28" x 41"

"I try to preserve yet modernize women's needlework by merging line, color and cloth.
I create a stylized line drawing and preview color choices on a computer. I stitch and
texture fabrics to convey luminosity and movement." Venues: La Jolla Festival of the Arts,
Contemporary Crafts Market San Francisco, The American Art Festival.

Jacqueline Mallegni

Bolinas, CA
www.mallegni.com • 415.868.2508

SKY BARGE I & II. Handmade paper, rattan, bamboo, willow. 28" x 18" x 72" each

"My work is about form and light—combining sculpture with illumination. Organic forms express the beauty and chaos around us, while the light emitted through the fibers of hand-made paper resonates in a familiar yet mysterious way." Venues: Claudia Chapline Gallery, Grounds for Sculpture, ACC San Francisco.

Susan McGehee

Manhattan Beach, CA
www.metalstrands.com • 310.545.4112

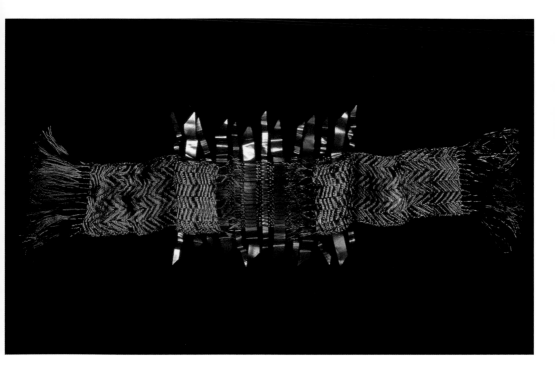

METALLIC SERENADE. Woven aluminum wire, copper. 15" x 38"

"I am a weaver who went to the hard stuff. I now weave only metals instead of fiber,
yet I still employ the same traditional tools, techniques and patterns. Weaving wire and
metals allows me to form pieces into dimensional shapes that retain form and vitality."
Venues: ACC San Francisco, Pinnacle Gallery, Elizabeth Doyle Gallery.

Melissa Woodburn

San Rafael, CA
mkwfineart@aol.com • 415.499.1655

ECHO OF THE SNAKE. Pine needle, clay, snake shed. 13" x 11" x 11"

"I am inspired by using a variety of media to express statements about the rhythms and cycles of living. The creative nature of the universe excites me and I filter this through my lens of female experience. I see the vessel as a metaphor for the temple of the soul."
Venues: Celebration of Craftswomen, Marin Open Studios, Marin Society of Artists.

Anne M. Austin

Alameda, CA
www.anneaustinstudios.com • 510.836.2663

TREES. Acrylic on wood. 12" x 14"

"My paintings and screens express a need to create something spontaneous and intriguing. The hard surface of wood allows me to create distinct, hard edges within the shapes. I use random brush strokes to build up layers of color and texture, trying not to fall into a pattern. Often, an abstract landscape simply appears."

PORTRAIT OF MY FATHER. Bastogne walnut, panga panga. 36" x 12"

"I create studio-made art furniture in exotic woods, joined without using store bought fasteners, and often finished with hand-rubbed oils to create a luster unmatchable with modern techniques." Venues: Gallery M, San Francisco Museum of Craft & Folk Art, ACC San Francisco.

Vesna Breznikar

Healdsburg, CA
www.vesnart.com • 707.433.2743

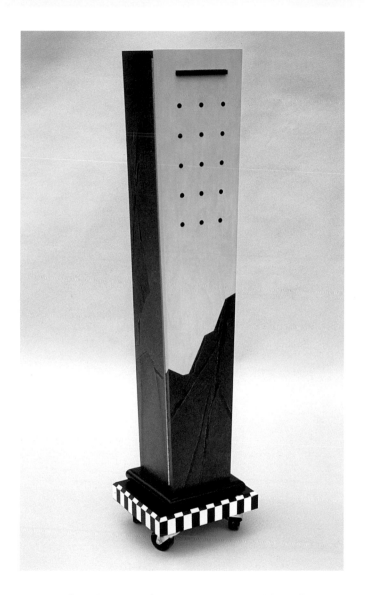

CD TOWER. Painted wood. 52" x 13" x 11"

"I love functional art. All everyday objects can be designed aesthetically, adding to function a measure of beauty. I design furniture to create sculptural and architectural forms. I paint furniture to celebrate color, emphasize form, and surprise the eye."
Venues: Gallery of Functional Art, The Artful Eye, Plaza Arts.

BOWL. Amboyna wood. 7" x 10"

"I produce bowls and vessels using burlwoods: redwood, buckeye, myrtle, olive, maple, manzanita and walnut from Northern California. I particularly love to make 'natural edge' bowls which offer wonderful sculptural effects." Venues: San Francisco International Gift Show, Highlights Gallery, One-Of-A-Kind Gallery.

Michael Hampel

Chelan, WA
www.hamneggs.biz • 509.687.6345

SHUTTER POD #1103. Persian walnut. 4.5" x 3.5"

"Trees have always inspired me. I try, through woodworking, to honor the beauty
and mystery of these beings—turning and sculpting are the closest way I've found. I
aim to reveal wood's infinite variations, whether polished smooth, textured or colored."
Venues: Best of the Northwest, Northwest Fine Woodworking Gallery, Sunburst Gallery.

Lynette Hunter

El Cajon, CA
lhunterstudio@aol.com • 619.208.6672

TEA POT. Buckeye burl, ebony. 8" x 10" x 6"

"I use wood as a canvas to create my art. My work consists of hollow vessels and wall hangings turned on a wood lathe. I am fascinated by the natural beauty of wood and specialize in exotic and burled woods from around the world." Venues: Sausalito Art Festival, Bellevue Art Museum Festival, Marin Art Festival.

Michael Kelley

La Habra, CA
kelley3@adelphia.net • 714.526.0276

BENTWOOD ROCKER. Maple, walnut. 44" x 28" x 36"

"An artistic rocking chair is a challenging piece of furniture to create. Designing a comfortable piece of furniture sets up an intriguing set of limitations that challenge my creativity as an artist. I think of my work as a fusion of contemporary art and furniture."
Venues: Kings Mountain Art Festival, Mill Valley Art Festival, La Quinta Art Festival.

WALL CABINET. Cherry, maple burl. 27" x 9" x 6"

"The merging of wood with other elements such as metal, paper, found objects, or wood in its 'raw' natural state allows me more freedom in the designing of a piece. On occasion I like to create pieces that are menacing, humorous, or perhaps functionally-impaired."
Venues: Design in Wood Show, Contemporary Arts Gallery.

HYBRID CHAIR. Walnut, rush fiber. 38" x 19" x 18"

"My work is mostly defined by function. The form comes from harmonizing
the materials within defined parameters. In this piece I wanted comfort,
durability and a simple elegance that does not immediately catch the eye."
Venues: Sonoma County Woodworkers Show, Mendocino Furniture Makers.

Bill Luce

Renton, WA
www.billluce.com • 425.277.6461

LUNAR LANDSCAPE #3. Holly. 6.5" x 10" x 11"

"The exploration of the quiet power of understated form is my main focus—
minimalism through refinement. I often use the movement of the wood itself
as it dries to infuse additional motion and spirit into deceptively simple forms."
Venues: Bellevue Art Museum Fair, Patina Gallery, Northwest Fine Woodworking.

Luci Lytle

San Diego, CA
luci@corrugatedart.com

MOSAIC SCREEN. Recycled corrugated fiber. 30" x 48"

"My passion is finding and using corrugated cardboard. As I discovered the quiet beauty of the corrugations and their subtle color palette, I created corrugated mosaics—abstract and symmetrical patterns which embellish functional pieces and, more recently, wall art and sculpture."

Mark Rehmar

O'Brien, OR
mail@mrstudio.com • 541.596.2393

TRIANGULAR TABLE. Curly maple, walnut, glass. 34" x 21" x 21"

"Both my furniture and multiple box series represent a constant balance in getting the feeling and function I want, while releasing the innate character of the figured woods and burl veneers I use—creating carefully detailed pieces, yet letting the wood speak for itself." Venue: ACC San Francisco.

COAT RACK, TABLE, MIRROR. Maple, walnut. 72" x 17", 29" x 34", 29" x 54"

"I make dynamic furniture that is fun to live with. I create curves by carving, steambending, laminating and vacuum forming. Choosing from the variety of colors and grain patterns further enhances the unique character of each piece." Venues: Sausalito Arts Festival, Bellevue Art Museum Show, Earthenworks Gallery.

Jon R. Swenson

Davis, CA
jswenson@dcn.org • 530.756.3297

SOJOURN. Maple, mahogany, alder, black walnut, rosewood. 13" x 15"

"I have always been fascinated by the juxtaposition of materials, and by questions of consciousness and creativity. My early preference for drawing and gesture can still be seen by close inspection. Lines are sketched, predicting joints; species are configured in a painterly way. Figures in the landscape reside in the annual rings."

Sandra Ortiz Taylor

San Francisco, CA
www.sandraortiztaylorart.com • 415.648.6826

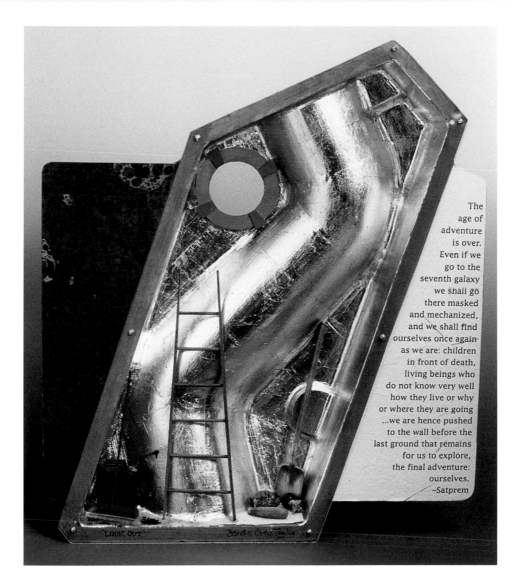

The
age of
adventure
is over.
Even if we
go to the
seventh galaxy
we shall go
there masked
and mechanized,
and we shall find
ourselves once again
as we are: children
in front of death,
living beings who
do not know very well
how they live or why
or where they are going
...we are hence pushed
to the wall before the
last ground that remains
for us to explore,
the final adventure:
ourselves.
—Satprem

LOOKOUT. Wood, silver leaf, hand-made paper. 14.5" x 12" x 2.75"

"My work frequently follows a narrative flow. Mixed media and *objet trouve*
combine to stimulate my small-scale sculptural works, collages, artist stamps
and artist books."

Alison Ulman

Oakland, CA
www.endlessprocess.com • 510.532.6179

SURREALIST COFFEE TABLE. Mahogany, bronze. 29" x 72" x 27"

"This is my 'Surrealist coffee table,' pre-arranged with magazines, books, even an album of memories carved from the sensuous mahogany; a tiny replica of the table itself lies upon the surface. I poised the table on bronze baby hands clutching balls in the French Provincial style. One ball has escaped!" Venues: SF Legion of Honor, LA Art Core.

Jay Younger

Beavercreek, OR
www.youngerwoodworks.com • 503.632.8222

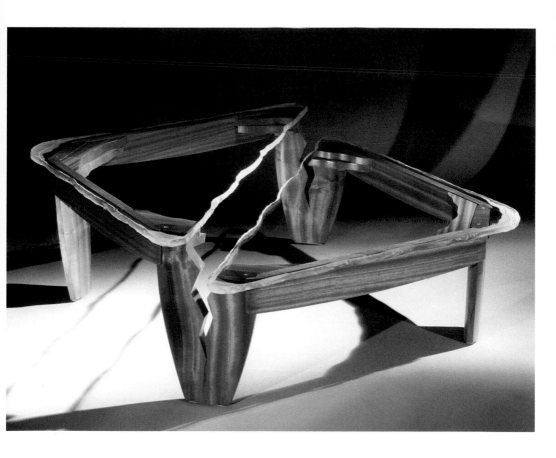

AFTER QUAKE. Sapele, sandblasted glass. 18" x 38" x 38"

"The fluid nature of my furniture designs provides a sense of movement and life. Using woods with unusual grains, I transform the design into unique, artistic furniture that respects elements of function and evokes joy." Venues: Sausalito Art Festival, Bellevue Art Museum Fair, Earthworks Galleries.

A New Leaf Gallery
Berkeley, CA 510.525.7621

ACC - American Craft Council
www.craftcouncil.org
San Francisco, CA - August
Baltimore, MD - February
St. Paul, MN - April

ACCI Gallery
Berkeley, CA 510.843.2527

Affaire in the Gardens
Beverly Hills, CA 310.550.4796

Alabaster
San Francisco, CA 415.558.0482

Allan Stone Gallery
New York, NY 212.987.1655

Alysia Duckler Gallery
Portland, OR 503.223.7595

American Art Festival
Sacramento, CA 775.832.6603

Andora Gallery
Carefree, AZ 480.595.1039

Andrea Schwartz Gallery
San Francisco, CA 415.495.2090

Anne Bradford Gallery
Healdsburg, CA 707.433.2808

Art & All That Jazz
Healdsburg, CA 707.433.7900

Art Concepts
Walnut Creek, CA 925.930.0157

Art in the Pearl
Portland, OR - August

Art in the Vineyard
Eugene, OR 541.345.1571

Art on Main Gallery
St. Helena, CA 707.963.3350

Artisan's Gallery
Mill Valley, CA 415.388.2044

ARTrails of Sonoma County
Santa Rosa, CA - October

ACGA Festivals
Assn. of Clay & Glass Artists
San Francisco, CA - May
Palo Alto, CA - July
www.acga.net

Atelier 31 Gallery
Seattle, WA 206.448.5250

Bainbridge Arts & Crafts
Bainbdg Isl., WA 206.842.3132

Baulines Craft Guild
CA Design Show, SF - May

Bellagio
Asheville, NC 828.277.8100

Bellevue Art Museum Fair
Bellevue, WA - July

Berkeley Open Studios
Berkeley, CA - Nov., Dec.

Best Bead Show
Tuscon, AZ crystalmyths.com

Best of the Northwest Fair
Seattle, WA - July

BKB & Company
Tacoma, WA 253.273.6884

Boca Museum of Art
Boca Raton, FL 561.392.2500

Bronze, Silver & Gold Gallery
Cambria, CA 805.927.5421

Buyers Market of Amer. Craft
Philadelphia, PA - Feb., July

Carlyn Gallerie
Dallas, TX 214.368.2828

Cecile Moochnek Gallery
Berkeley, CA 510.549.1018

Celebration of Craftswomen
S. Francisco, CA - November

Celebration of Fine Art
Scottsdale, AZ 480.443.7695

CFA Gallery
San Anselmo, CA 415.457.8847

Chambers Gallery
Cambria, CA 805.927.9445

Claudia Chapline Gallery
Stinson Beach, CA 415.868.2308

Clay Hands
Tubac, AZ 520.398.2885

Cohen Rese Gallery
San Francisco, CA 415.781.6440

Concepts Gallery
Carmel, CA 831.624.0661

ConneXtions
30 Princess Ct. @ Bridgeway
Sausalito, CA 415.332.1486
www.connextionsgallery.com

*A mixed media gallery
emphasizing locally-made,
moderately priced new work.*

Contemporary Crafts Market
Santa Monica, CA - June
San Francisco, CA - March
415.995.4925
www.craftsource.org

Contemp. Crafts Museum
Portland, OR 503.223.2654

CraftBoston
Boston, MA - May

De Novo
Palo Alto, CA 650.327.1256

Design in Wood Show
San Diego, CA - June

Deva
Winst-Salem, OR 336.723.4022

Dolby Chadwick
San Francisco, CA 415.956.3560

Dolphin Gallery
Kansas City, MO 816.842.5877

Dovetail Collection
Healdsburg, CA 707.431.0111

Dunn-Mehler Gallery
Hf. Moon Bay, CA 650.726.7667

Earthenworks Gallery
Prt. Townsd.,WA 360.385.0328

Earthworks
Los Altos, CA 650.948.5141

Earthworks Gallery
Yachats, OR 541.547.4300

East Bay Open Studios
Oakland, CA - June

Elizabeth Doyle Gallery
Maui, HI 808.879.0092

Eriksen Gallery
Hf. Moon Bay, CA 650.726.1598

Exploding Head Gallery
Sacamento, CA 916.442.8424

FiberScene.com
San Francisco, CA

Fireworks Gallery
Halifax, N. Scotia 800.720.gems

Freddie Fong Gallery
San Francisco, CA 415.391.6133

Freehand
Los Angeles, CA 323.655.2607

Fresh Paint Art Advisors
Culver City, CA 310.558.9355

Fusion Gallery
Ashland,OR 541.552.9285

Gallery 33
Portland, OR 503.219.9600

Gallery M
Denver, CO 877.331.8401

Gallery of Jewels
San Francisco, CA 415.285.0626

Gallery OneZero
San Francisco, CA 415.989.9157

George Billis Gallery
New York, NY 212.645.2621

George Krevsky Gallery
San Francisco, CA 415.397.9748

Glass Artists Gallery
Bellevue, WA 877.320.0800

Graton Gallery
Graton, CA 707.829.8912

Greenwood Chebithes Gall.
Laguna Bch., CA 949.494.0669

Grounds for Sculpture
Hamilton, NJ 609.586.0616

Gumps
San Francisco, CA 800.822.8055

Hang Art
Palo Alto, CA hangart.com

Headlands Ctr. for the Arts
Sausalito, CA 415.331.2787

Hibberd/McGrath Gallery
Brecknrdg., CO 970.453.6391

Highlands Sculpture Gallery
Carmel,CA 831.624.0535

Highlight Gallery
Mendocino, CA 707.937.3132

Home Comfort Fine Art
Sedro Wlly., WA 360.854.9280

ARTSPAN
sf open studios

Visit the studios of 900 artists !

Each weekend in October, San Francisco artists open their workspaces to the public.

www.sfopenstudios.com
(415) 861-9838

Artwork left to right and top to bottom is by Kathleen Maley, Beth Weintraub, Carlo Abruzze, Diane Rollins Feissel, Vince Meyer, Rob Costin, Tim Baskerville, Delisa, Melissa Wagner, and Michael Markowitz.

Howard Mandville Gallery
Kirkland, WA 425.889.8212

Hunters Point Open Studios
San Francisco, CA - May

ICB Building Shows
Sausalito, CA - June, Dec.

Indian Wells Arts Festival
Palm Desert, CA - April

Iota Gallery
Dallas, TX 214.522.2999

JFK Video Installation
New York, NY British Airways

John Natsoulas Gallery
Davis, CA 530.756.3938

Joyce Gordon Gallery
Oakland, CA 510.465.8928

Judah Magnes Museum
Berkeley, CA 510.549.6950

Karan Ruhlen Gallery
Santa Fe, NM 505.820.0807

Kathryn Markel Fine Arts
New York, NY 212.366.5368

Katonah Museum of Art
Katonah, NY 914.232.9555

Kings Mountain Art Fair
Woodside, CA - September

KPFA Community Crafts Fair
San Francisco, CA - December

LA Art Core
Los Angeles, CA laartcore.org

La Jolla Festival of the Arts
La Jolla, CA - June

La Quinta Arts Festival
San Diego, CA - March

Lafayette Gallery
Lafayette, CA 925.284.2788

Laguna Art Museum
L. Beach, CA 949.494.8971

LaKae Gallery
Scottsdale, AZ 480.874.2624

Left Bank Gallery
Wellfleet, MA 508.349.9451

LIMN Gallery
San Francisco, CA 415.977.1300

Linda Fairchild Contemp. Art
San Francisco, CA 415.296.5191

Lyons Head Gallery
Carmel Val., CA 831.659.4192

Magnolia Gallery
Larkspur, CA 415.924.7702

Marin Arts Festival
Civic Ctr. Lagoon Pk. - June
Mill Valley, CA 415.388.0151
www.marinartfestival.com

*Meet 250 master artists at
the show best representing
the character of Marin.*

Marin Open Studios
Marin County, CA - May

Marin Society of Artists
Ross, CA 415.454.9561

Mendocino Furniture Makers
Fort Bragg, CA

Mill Valley Fall Art Festival
Mill Valley, CA - September

Museum of Arts & Design
New York, NY 212.956.3535

Museum of Craft & Folk Art
San Francisco, CA 415.775.0991

Museum of Glass
Tacoma, WA 253.396.1768

NaPua Gallery
Maui, HI 808.874.0510

New Masters Gallery
Carmel, CA 800.336.4014

NextMonet.com
San Francisco, CA 888.914.5050

NW Fine Woodworking
Bellevue, WA 425.462.5382

NW Flower & Garden Show
Seattle, WA 206.789.5333

NW Museum of Art & Culture
Spokane, WA 509.456.3931

Oakland Museum Cltr.s Gallery
Oakland, CA 510.834.2296

Packard Reath Gallery
Lewes, DE 302.644.7513

Palo Alto Festival of the Arts
Palo Alto, CA 650.324.3121

Patina Gallery
Santa Fe, NM 505.986.3432

Pieces Gallery
Healdsburg, CA 707.433.3233

Pinnacle Gallery
Phoenix, AZ 480.563.9800

Plaza Arts Gallery
Healdsburg, CA 707.433.1970

Point Reyes Open Studios
Point Reyes, CA - November

Portland Rose Festival
Portland, OR - June

Quicksilver Mine Co.
Forestville, CA 707.887.0799

"Where the local arts reside"

810 Main Street, Martinez, Ca. 94553

925.229.8281

shakeyhandgallery@sbcglobal.net

Racine Art Museum
Racine, WI www.ramart.org

Reflections Gallery
Cannon Bch., OR 503.436.8852

Rhodes Stringfellow
Cannon Bch., OR 503.436.8520

Richmond Art Center
Richmond, CA 510.620.6772

Ryan Gallery
Lincoln City, OR 541.994.5391

Sacramento Art Festival
Sacramento, CA - October

Salem Art Festival
Salem, OR - July

SF African Amer. Hist. Society
San Francisco, CA 415.441.0640

San Francisco Art Expo
Ft. Mason Center - January
San Francisco, CA 312.587.3300
www.sfiae.com

*Featuring over 100 galleries
representing an eclectic
array of modern artwork.*

San Francisco Intl. Gift Fair
San Francisco, CA - February

San Francisco Legion of Honor
San Francisco, CA thinker.org

San Francisco Open Studios
Throughout the city - October
San Francisco, CA 415.861.9838
www.sfopenstudios.com

*ArtSpan builds connections
within San Francisco's visual
arts community.*

SFMOMA Artists Gallery
San Francisco, CA 415.441.4777

SFMOMA Museum Store
San Francisco, CA 415.357.4035

Sandra Ainsley Gallery
Toronto, Ontario 416.362.4480

Sausalito Art Festival
Sausalito, CA - September

Sculpture to Wear
Santa Monica, CA 310.829.9960

Seattle Art Museum Gallery
Seattle, WA 206.654.3231

Seattle Gift Show
Seattle, WA - January

Serendipity
LaConner, WA 360.466.1620

Settler's West Gallery
Tucson, AZ settlerswest.com

Shakey Hand Gallery
Martinez, CA 925.229.8281

Shamwari Gallery
Oakland, CA 510.923.1222

Shockley Designs
Mariposa, CA 209.966.3122

Silicon Valley Open Studios
Silicon Valley, CA - May

Skirball Cultural Center
Los Angeles, CA skirball.com

Smithsonian Craft Show
Washington, DC - April

Solomon Dubnick Gallery
Sacramento, CA 916.920.4547

Sonoma Co. Woodworkers
sonomawoodworkers.com

Southern Exposure
San Francisco, CA 415.863.2141

Spectrum Studio
Spokane, WA 509.747.5267

SPIE Conferences
San Jose, CA www.spie.org

Spokane ArtFest
Spokane, WA - May

Starfish Gallery
Victoria, BC starfishglass.bc.ca

Steel Gallery
San Francisco, CA 415.885.1655

Studio 7 Fine Arts
Pleasanton, CA 925.846.4322

Switzer Gallery
Tiburon, CA 415.789.5289

Tag Gallery
Nashville, TN 615.298.2905

Tercera Gallery
24 N. Santa Cruz Avenue
Los Gatos, CA 408.354.9484
www.terceragallery.com

*Contemporarty art, studio
furniture, & jewelry by estab-
lished & emerging artists.*

The American Arts Festival
Incline Vill., NV 775.832.6603

The Artful Eye
Calistoga, CA 707.942.4743

The Blue Studio
San Francisco, CA 415.577.8126

The Gardner
Berkeley, CA 510.548.4545

The Southwest Art Forum
Indio, CA - January

Thomas Reynolds Gallery
San Francisco, CA 415.441.4093

Toomey Tourell Fine Art
San Francisco, CA 415.989.6444

Topeo Gallery
New Hope, PA 215.862.2750

Valley Art Gallery
San Francisco, CA 925.935.4311

Velvet Da Vinci
508 Hayes Street @ Octavia
San Francisco, CA 415.626.7478
www.velvetdavinci.com

*Representing over fifty studio
jewelry artists from the Bay
Area and around the world.*

Verdigris Clay Studio & Gallery
2801 Leavenworth @ Beach
San Francisco, CA 415.440.2898
www.verdigrisgallery.com

*Verdigris offers a collection
of fine ceramic art featuring
over thirty Bay Area artists.*

Verne Collection
Cleveland, OH 216.231.8866

Virgil Gallery
Nevada City, CA 530.265.5790

V. Breier Gallery
San Francisco, CA 415.929.7173

Virtual Art Solutions
Beverly Hills, CA 310.859.0579

William Zimmer Gallery
Mendocino, CA 707.937.5121

WORKS Gallery
Philadelphia, PA 215.938.2176

Worth Ryder Gallery
Berkeley, CA 510.642.2582

Worthington Gallery
Springdale, UT 435.772.3446

Youngman Gallery
Calistoga, CA 800.551.0585

Zado Gallery
Portland, OR 503.781.5545

Zapature Gallery
Portland, OR 503.970.9443

Zosaku
Berkeley, CA 510.524.7404

ARTIST INDEX

PART ONE: 2-D

PAINTING
DRAWING
PRINTMAKING
PHOTOGRAPHY

4....Alexander
5....Amavisca
6....Amit
7....Archer
8....Auster
9....Blau
10....Bolingbroke
11....Bording
12....Brown
13....Buffalo
14....Carr
15....Chao
16....Chlouber
17....Cole
18....Confer
19....Cootsona
20....D'Amico
21....Davidson
22....Denevan
23....Diaman
24....Erickson
25....Evenson
26....Friedlander
27....Gawlowski
28....Gibbons
29....Gibson
30....Gleeson
31....Gonzalez
32....Gruber
33....Hahn
34....Hamel
35....Hancock

36....Hayakawa
37....Hensley
38....Herschend
39....Hopkins
40....Howe
41....Hundt
42....Jardel
43....Jucker
44....Keller
45....Kennedy
46....Klahn
47....Kramer
48....Lack
49....Lord
50....Lydon
51....Lynch
52....Maddox
53....Maher
54....Manchester
55....Mandel
56....Mark
57....Marlo
58....Martinez
59....Maxwell
60....McAbery
61....McCarthy
62....McIlrath
63....Miki
64....Miller
65....Minden
66....Morgan
67....Nilsson
68....Ogren
69....Paster
70....Patt
71....Phill
72....Pickern
73....Plistermann
74....Poloto
75....Printis

76.....Przewodek
77.....Ramos
78.....Ratcliff
79.....Romaine
80.....Sandbo
81.....Slater
82.....Solinsky
83.....Steiner
84.....Switzer
85.....Tocher
86.....Turner
87.....Varney
88.....Vliek
89.....Willis
90.....Wilson
91.....Young

PART TWO: 3-D

CERAMICS

92.....Albrechtsen
93.....Barnett
94.....Burton
95.....Conrow
96.....Crain
97.....Deist
98.....Downing
99.....Felix
100....Goldenberg
101....Gooding
102....Grimm
103....Keiser
104....Klinger
105....Lawson
106....Lipkin
107....MacKenzie
108....McNeely
109....Meade
110....Miyagi
111....Morales
112....Pallie

113....Pearce
114....Pool
115....Porter
116....Post
117....Purcell
118....Reynolds
119....Roberts
120....Schachter
121....Standhardt
122....Vrana & Miller
123....Wax & Bing

GLASS

124....Bazaz
125....Bergsma
126....Cantor
127....Cotton
128....Ferrera
129....Gilula
130....Jones
131....King-Lehman
132....Lindemann
133....Lindsay
134....Newman
135....Pizzichillo
       & Gordon
136....Webster

JEWELRY

137....Bettencourt
138....Driver
139....Faust
140....Goldsmith
141....Goodenough
142....Izzi
143....Jones
144....Kneeland
145....Kupke-Peyla
146....Lamberti
147....Macdonald
148....McGuinness

149....Naumburg
150....Ronay

METAL

151....Borchardt
152....Bowman
153....Cantor-Fallihee
154....Gard
155....Hermes
156....Irish
157....Jacobs
158....Marson
159....Slovis
160....Valdes
161....Wilbur

TEXTILES

162....Durham
163....Hirota
164....Mallegni
165....McGehee
166....Woodburn

WOOD

167....Austin
168....Bellini
169....Breznikar
170....DeVore
171....Hampel
172....Hunter
173....Kelley
174....Kirby
175....Leighton
176....Luce
177....Lytle
178....Rehmar
179....Rolland
180....Swenson
181....Taylor
182....Ulman
183....Younger

PHOTO CREDITS

Azadphoto.com	141
Mustafa Balil	176
Blackcat Studios	105
John Brennan	120
Steve Buckley	163
Kate Cameron	99, 177
Philip Cohen	181
Brandi Easter	111
Lee Fatherree	119, 135
Donald J. Felton	102
Courtney Frisse	106
Kim Harrington	153
Robert Hermes	155
Nick Jahn	101
Ron Jaffe	179
Dan Kvitka	161
Tom Liden	123
Brian Mahany	98
Jerry McCollum	125
Thomas Minczeski	167
Andrew Newhart	165
Richard Nicol	124
Dennis O'Neil	169
Piro Patton	164
Spencer Paul	129
Cindy Pavlinac	162
George Post	109,114, 116, 146, 158
Hap Sakwa	95,112,115, 127, 124, 137, 133, 138, 139, 142, 143, 145, 147, 148, 150, 170
Frank Schellenberg	157
Roger Schrieber	134
J. Wallen	159

San Francisco international art exposition
at Fort Mason Center

www.sfiae.com

A project of Thomas Blackman Associates, 230 West Huron, Chicago, IL 60610, phone 312.587.3300, fax 312.587.3304